THE ECHO OF GREECE

BOOKS BY EDITH HAMILTON

THE GREEK WAY

THE ROMAN WAY

THREE GREEK PLAYS

MYTHOLOGY

WITNESS TO THE TRUTH

SPOKESMEN FOR GOD

THE ECHO OF GREECE

EDITH HAMILTON

The
ECHO OF
GREECE

W · W · NORTON & COMPANY · INC ·
NEW YORK

Contents

THE ECHO OF GREECE

"Whose distant footsteps echo
Through the corridors of time"

LONGFELLOW

Introduction

FOURTH century Athens is completely overshadowed by Athens of the fifth century, so much so that it is little considered. Any brief history of Greece will more likely than not end with Athens' defeat in the Peloponnesian War in 404 B.C. There will be references, perhaps, to Demosthenes and Philip of Macedon and Alexander the Great, all too important to be omitted, but no account of the time they lived in will be thought necessary. Real interest in Greece ceases with Sparta's victory over Athens. Plato and Aristotle live in a timeless world of philosophy without any local habitation, and are hardly thought of as Greeks but as intellectual forces.

And yet, their century, the fourth century, has a special claim on our attention apart from the great men it produced, for it is the prelude to the end of Greece, not only of her glory, but of her life historically. Greek genius did not come to an end, but it took a new direc-

9

tion in new places. Science and mathematics went on to triumphs in Greek colonies and in foreign cities crowded with the Greeks Alexander had set traveling away from home, but none came back to Greece and to Athens. Not one really great name relieves the blankness.

The fourth century is the introduction to a world-tragedy, the disappearance of creative power in Greece. With its close there is an end of the art and philosophy which have made a few centuries in Athens more precious to the West than many ages in many countries. The years which ushered in this loss to the world never to be replaced have a unique importance.

During the century that follows, Athens drops out of history. Two famous schools are founded, the Stoics and the Epicureans, but they are the last flaming up of Greek genius in Greece until Plutarch appears more than three hundred years later when the ancient world was passing away.

Plutarch was such a voluminous writer and so much of what he wrote has come down to us that in addition to the wealth of historical information his Lives give us, we can construct a personal history of him and his circle as of no other Greek. If only we could do that for Plato and Aristotle about whom we know almost nothing personal. And yet it is true that Plutarch, so essentially Greek as he is, can help us to understand the heterogeneous collection of fourth-century Athens' great men.

We know all Greeks better through him, Plato as well
as Menander.

With him the Greek spirit has a brief renaissance
which ends with the two greatest Stoics, Epictetus, the
slave, and Marcus Aurelius, the emperor, both of whom
wrote in Greek although the one was Roman bred and
the other Roman born and bred. The explanation usually
given for their doing so is that by then it had become a
popular fashion in Rome to speak Greek, but that was
not a consideration likely to influence either man. They
wrote in Greek because they wanted to express Greek
thoughts, and they were the last to do so. The Greek
Fathers of the Church were caught up in doctrinal disputes foreign to the Greek way of thinking. The shadow
of the Dark Ages already lay upon them and they were
not able to see what was unimportant. They could not
grasp the Greek way of thinking. Of all the leaders in
the early church St. Augustine alone made an approach
to it. After him it died and for many hundreds of years
it had no resurrection. It took no share in the all-
important process going on during those ages, the
growth of the Church to supreme power. Rome was
master and there was no place for the spirit of Socrates
and Plato and Plutarch. The terrible *odium theologicum*
which for centuries distracted Christendom would have
been unimaginable to all three of them.

Theological hatred is based on a totalitarian rule

over men's minds and spirits which Socrates and the others would have viewed with abhorrence. To them as to all Greeks freedom was first in importance. Fundamental to everything the Greeks achieved was their conviction that good for humanity was possible only if men were free, body, mind, and spirit, and if each man limited his own freedom. A good state or work of art or piece of thinking was possible only through the self-mastery of the free individual, self-government.

Chapter I

FREEDOM

IN THE early fifth century B.C. when the Age of Pericles still lay in the future, Western civilization reached a crossroads. Greece was confronted with an ever dreaded danger becoming a fact. A great Eastern power was on the march to invade her. To the Greeks peril from the East was a perpetual menace. They traced it back to the old story of Helen's being carried off to Troy and the Greek ships following her. That clash between East and West in which the West invaded the East was, the Greeks believed, the first act in a tragic conflict which could have no end. East and West were natural antagonists, and no defeat of the East could ever be final in the vast stretches of Asia overflowing with treasure and with men.

Now the curtain had risen for another act. The Homeric roles were reversed, and the East was attacking the West. Persia, then the great Asiatic power, was advancing with vast armies and vast fleets upon a little country with no vast supplies of anything material.

Western civilization at that time meant Greece. Egypt had fallen into powerless decay; Rome was slowly subduing Italy with no thought to give to the East; Carthage and her colonies, the third great power of the day, belonged in·spirit not to the West, but the East. They were outposts of Asia. The protagonists were Greece and Persia. The little Greek nation faced the Orient. It was a case of the pygmy and the giant, but the pygmy drove the giant back. It was a miracle, every Greek knew, brought about by heroism. There was little danger that the men who fought at Marathon and Salamis would deny the force of the spirit and turn to the material. As the Greeks at Salamis after the battle watched the Persian fleet depart, Themistocles said, "It is not we who have done this." Spiritual force had triumphed over the greatest material forces ever yet assembled, and the result was the triumph of the spirit in Periclean Athens.

To the Greeks of that day their most precious possession, freedom, was the distinguishing mark between East and West. Despotism was the form of rule in the East. Despots, as far as the Greeks knew them — there were none in their part of the world — always acted in the same way, clearing the road to the throne by exterminating the royal family, shedding blood without measure, using any means to forward their ends, and generally successful in increasing enormously for a time the power of the state. They did not enslave the people for they were already slaves, helpless masses at the ruler's disposal. Aristotle spoke for Greece when he said that Asiatics were slaves by nature. "You do not know what freedom is," Herodotus reports a Greek saying to a Persian. "If you did you would fight for it with bare hands if you had no weapons."

In the magnificent empires of the ancient world, Egypt, Babylon, Assyria, Persia, during their thousands of years of civilization, freedom was unknown, un-thought-of. It was not until their foundations were fall-ing that the idea dawned in men's minds. The country where it was born was fundamentally unoriental in ways of life and thought and was to set its mark permanently on the West.

The ancient civilizations were alike in one respect, in a refusal to recognize limits. Exaggeration was stamped upon them, a rejection of the limits of reality. It is plain to see in their art, in the monstrous Assyrian bird-and-beast statues, in the pyramids and the colossal images and the tremendous temples of Egypt, in the hanging gardens of Babylon. It is apparent, too, in the showers of bar-baric pearl and gold, the heaped-up treasures on one hand and the wretched, helpless multitudes on the other, incredible magnificence side by side with incredible squalor. Eastern life was lived at extremes.

Freedom, the power to live under one's own control and not another's, is unthinkable in such an atmosphere. Unlimited freedom is chaos. It would destroy mankind. Any order, by whatever means, is preferable. The East had an endless succession of despotisms because it never conceived of order in any other way. The West discovered a way to order through freedom. It was a Greek discovery. Why the idea came to a little country poor and sparsely settled, and not to majestic Egypt or Babylon the Great may seem at first sight strange, but the reason is not hard to find. It lies in the very nature of freedom. Freedom was born in Greece because there men limited their own freedom.

Fundamental in the Greeks was their conviction that limits were good. Exaggeration was foreign to them. They detested extremes and the idea of the limitless repelled them. Greek words which meant boundless, illimitable, and the like, had a bad connotation. Not only the everyday men but the thinkers and the artists all kept a firm hold on reality. Homer's gods were not transcendent mysteries, but comfortably real personages who lived and acted just the way the Greeks did. The Greeks did not want the transcendental and the mysterious. They wanted the truth and they never thought it could be found by escaping from the real. Greek art at its best and most characteristic is kept within the limits of the real world. Not the winged, but the wing-

less, victory is truly representative. The Greek artist
instinctively turned away from the strange. He would
have nothing to do with the eccentric or even the acci-
dental. He was searching for what has permanent meaning. He was trying to express something fundamental
and universal in everything he made whether it was a
temple or a statue or a vase. The Assyrian artist produced
what he pleased without a thought of fundamentals and
universals. He swept limits aside in his portentous images.
His imagination was free to wander where it would. But
the Greek artist had no wish for that kind of freedom.
He knew a law which he was constrained to obey.
Montesquieu said, "Laws are necessary relations springing from the nature of things." It is a statement essentially
Greek. The ruling characteristic of the Greeks was
that they were driven to find out the necessary relations,
the clues that lead from confusion into order.

The young men of the Parthenon frieze were not
copies of real men the artist knew; they were not por-
traits of individuals, but they were not purely imaginary
creations. They had more than natural human beauty;
nevertheless they were natural human beings. They were
the expression of the artist's discovery of the necessary
relation between beauty and truth. He sought as much
as the philosopher, as much as the scientist, for the essential idea which gives meaning and order to the discordant
and confused mass of details in the actual world. He dis-

covered a harmony underlying the opposition between body and soul which was to become so acute in the world after Greece. He found a form to express the union of spirit and flesh, the divine shown in the human, physical perfection which evoked the sense of spiritual perfection.

What the artist did in his field the statesman did in his. He found the necessary relation between law and freedom. Thucydides makes Pericles say, "We are a free democracy, but we obey the laws, more especially those which protect the oppressed and the unwritten laws whose transgression brings shame." Willing obedience to law written and unwritten made the Athenians free and the clear implication in Pericles' words is that they thought the latter, the unwritten, were the most important. The fact has deep significance for the first self-government in the world. Pericles knew and the audience he was speaking to knew that most of the written laws, the laws on the statute books, as for instance the laws against murder and robbery, were without effect upon the vast majority who had never an impulse to commit the one or the other, but the unwritten laws whose violation brings no court sentence or prison term made a direct claim upon every one of them. Obedience to what Professor Whitehead has called the unenforceable, that to which no force can compel, the Athenian accepted as the basic condition of freedom for men living

together, obedience to kindness and compassion and un-
selfishness and all the long list of qualities without which
life would be intolerable except to a hermit in a desert.
The limits to action established by law were a mere
nothing compared to the limits established by a man's
free choice.

This conception of what freedom means dawned
upon the Greeks. The quality they valued most — the
Greek word is *sophrosuné* — cannot be expressed by
any single English word. It is oftenest translated by self-
control, but it meant more than that. It was the spirit
behind the two great Delphic sayings, "Know thyself"
and "Nothing in excess." Arrogance, insolent self-asser-
tion, was of all qualities most detested by the Greeks.
Sophrosuné was the exact opposite. It had its nature, as
Aristotle would say, in the excellent and it meant accepting the bounds excellence laid down for human nature,
restraining impulses to unrestricted freedom, shunning
excess, obeying the inner laws of harmony and propor-
tion. This was the virtue the Greeks esteemed beyond
all others not because they were moderate lovers of the
golden mean, but because their spontaneity and ever-
changing variety and ardent energy of life had to have
the strong control of a disciplined spirit or end in sense-
less violence.

That was the Greek ideal, and the result was their
freedom. The idea that only the man who holds himself

within self-chosen limits can be free is one of their great legacies to us.

Through *sophrosuné* Greece discovered how men could live together in freedom, and she expressed her discovery by creating the first self-government in the world. An insignificant little town in a small and poverty-poor country made the discovery under the leadership of a single man. It was back in the early sixth century, more than a hundred years before Athens' great day, that a bold and far-thinking statesman, Solon, conceived the idea of a completely new kind of state, in which all citizens would have an active share and all would be equal before the law. When he laid the foundation of it in Athens, free government came into the world. It was an experiment which could have been tried only in Athens where the new was always attractive, a most unusual spirit to animate a people. It was a marked peculiarity of Athens. The disposition of the explorer distinguished her from other places. Ways never trodden before allured her. Athens kept that spirit for a long time. St. Luke, writing some six hundred years later, said, "The Athenians spend their time on nothing else but to tell or to hear some new thing."

They were ready to listen to the new thing Solon had to tell them and follow him along a way no country had ever trod. The experiment which had never even been conceived of elsewhere was carried out not by

warriors drawn up in battle array as at Runnymede, not
by terror and the guillotine as in France, but peacefully,
in some Athenian Independence Hall where the Founding Fathers of the new republic assembled to be convinced by one of the greatest statesmen the world has
known. Only in diminutive Attica of which Athens was
the capital would the new idea have been carried out.
Greece had indeed long before come forward in ways
of thought as well as ways of art. Science had been born
in Greek towns at the end of the Mediterranean, and
men were thinking as well not only about the universe,
but about themselves as different from others, individuals,
not indistinguishable human masses. The rights of man
followed inevitably in a town like Athens with a man
like Solon to guide her, but only the Athenians were
able to take that step. The other Greek towns ruled the
country around them. In Attica every farmer, shepherd,
craftsman, was a citizen, taking part in the government
and in the courts of justice.

At this point slavery, universal in the world then,
confronts the readers. Many men in Athens had no share
in the rights of man, but no one ever gave a thought to
slaves, no more in the West than in the East. Everywhere
the way of life depended on them. One cannot say that
they were accepted as such, for there was no acceptance.
Everyone used them; no one paid any attention to them.
Solon's new idea of political and legal rights for every

man was not disturbed by any revolutionary notion cropping up about slaves being men. They were really not men. Solon believed with complete conviction that the poorest and lowliest citizen in Attica had the right of and the capacity for self-rule, but slaves never entered his brilliantly daring and constructive mind. It should not be difficult for us to bring together the contented slave-owner and the statesman whose deep concern was to give the lowliest a share in the government. The early American republic which declared that all men are created free and equal admitted slave-owning states. When the Greek achievement is considered, what must be remembered is that the Greeks were the first who thought about slavery. To think about it was to condemn it, and by the end of the second century, two thousand years before our Civil War, the great school of the Stoics, most widely spread of Greek philosophies, was denouncing it as an intolerable wrong.

At least the Athenian citizen had true freedom. There has never been a state more free; there have been few as free. Never was freedom of speech restricted; not in times of utmost peril when an enemy was advancing to the very walls of the city. Even then the blunders and failures of politicians and generals were shown up in the theatre as well as discussed by whoever chose; even then at the opening of the Assembly, the ultimate power made up of every Athenian, the presiding officer asked, "Does any one wish to speak?"

Once an Athenian army far from home and surrounded by greatly superior forces had to try to break through them as a last chance. Their leader made a short speech before they started. "You live," he told them, "in the only free city in the world. In Athens alone the state does not interfere with a man's daily life." "The individual can be trusted," Thucydides reports Pericles as saying. "Let him alone." "The capacity of mankind for self-government," a statesman, Athenian in spirit, phrased it around the year 1776 A.D. No doubt James Madison had never an idea that he was speaking Greek. Athens and Solon were not in even the farthest background of his mind, but, as Aristotle said, the excellent becomes the permanent. Once seen it is never completely lost. Somewhere in this or that man's thought it lives though forgotten in the world of action, and one can never be sure that it is not on the point of breaking out into action, only sure that it will do so sometime.

Chapter II

ATHENS' FAILURE

"THE KIND of events that once took place will by reason of human nature take place again." So Thucydides wrote at the end of the Peloponnesian War and the end of the great age of Athens. The kind of events that took place in the first free nation of the world may by reason of this unchanging human nature be repeated in the modern world. The course that Athens followed can be to us not only a record of old unhappy far-off things, but a blueprint of what may happen again. Greek art and Greek philosophy are acknowledged to be living influences today, but Greek political thinking is passed over. Nevertheless it was one of their great contributions. They thought profoundly about politics, and as in every other field they entered they made discoveries which are forever significant. Freedom was a Greek discovery.

In the fifth century B.C. Athens showed what free men living and working together can bring to pass. She achieved the balance between freedom and union, between the individual and the community. In her distant past as in all antiquity the individual's welfare was completely subordinated to the common welfare. If the harvest failed the fields could be watered with human blood. Any one could be put to death for any purpose to do good to the tribe. But slowly the importance of each human being increased. In time laws were passed to defend the individual against the community as well as the other way about, and finally in Athens the height was reached when men who were no longer sacrificed to whatever was thought a benefit to the state, voluntarily sacrificed themselves for its welfare. Athenians were free and they used their freedom to serve their city.

They showed what miracles can be brought about when people willingly work together for the good of all. Every Athenian as a matter of course gave time and effort to building and lifting up the common life. Thucydides makes Pericles say: "We are a free democracy. ... We do not allow absorption in our own affairs to interfere with participation in the city's. We regard the man who holds aloof from public affairs as useless; nevertheless we yield to none in independence of spirit and complete self-reliance."

Men who loved independence and wanted to rely on themselves thought of public affairs as being their own responsibility; the reason was that they saw clearly

outlined against the darkness of the world around them
what Athens was to each one of them, the bulwark of
safety in a dangerous world, the city of freedom in a
world of despotic rulers and slavish subjects, and they
were no more willing to leave her in the hands of other
people than they would have been to turn their private
interests over to others. An Athenian wanted to be and
was a practical politician. Solon's foundation was wisely
built upon during the years, and when the great test
came with the invasion of Greece by Persia it stood firm.
Athens took the lead in the desperate decision to resist
and give battle to the immense forces of the Orient, and
all alone, with no help from the other Greeks, she won
the victory of Marathon, still incredible to us today, and
forced the mighty host to depart.

In the final defeat of the Persians at Salamis ten
years later, Athens, though no longer alone, was the leader
and there was a wonderful outburst of patriotic devotion. Athenians saw their city as the one that had proved
beyond all others that the power of the spirit could be
stronger than the power of overwhelmingly great physical forces. She was the abode of "Excellence, much
labored for by the sons of men," said Aristotle. An
Athenian must be more excellent than other Greeks. So
the men of the early Periclean age saw their city. Pericles bade them gaze at her until they were filled with love
for her, for her humanity and self-restraint, for her free-

dom founded in law, for her service to the things of the mind which made her what Pericles called her, "the School of Hellas."

Herodotus, himself no Athenian, testifies to the esteem she was held in by the other Greeks. "Of all Greeks," he says, "the Athenians stood first for wisdom." "Athens when she was ruled by tyrants was no better than her neighbors. When free she was by far the first of all." Even better testimony is given by the fact that soon after the Persian defeat a number of cities chose her to be their leader, an extraordinary action on the part of Greeks. But a wonderful new idea of Greek union had dawned, full of promise for the world. There had never before been anything like it. Greeks were fiercely independent by nature and every city feared and distrusted every other. Only the extreme peril of the Persian invasion could have forced them to come together, but that showed them what union could do. Soon after the defeat a league of free cities came into being, all equal partners, all bound to forward each other's interests. Athens was elected to head it for the reason, Herodotus explains, that she was known from earliest times as the liberator of men.

One cannot but wonder what would have happened if the league had succeeded and spread to the rest of Greece. What could not a united Greece have done? Even when she was split into little quarreling segments

she outstripped all the ancient world and in many ways
the modern world. What might not the West have advanced to if Greece, not Rome, had been the leader?
But the hope of a United States of Greece came to
nothing. The Athenian League failed and the reason was
that Athens failed. Her position as the head of the
league gave her power; and the greed for more power
which, Thucydides insists throughout his history, all
power creates, overcame her excellence. In a few years
she had forgotten the ideals that had saved her from
Persia, her devotion to freedom, her spirit of self-
restraint. She turned the league of free cities into a
league of unwilling subjects to herself. Men called her
now not the Liberator, but the Tyrant City. In Thucydides Pericles says to the Athenians: "You have an empire
to lose and a danger to face from those whom your imperial rule has made to hate you." The result was the
Peloponnesian War which lasted twenty-seven years and
put an end to Athens' great age.

Greed caused the war, Thucydides says. Both
Athens and Sparta were aggressors; each wanted what
the other had. Thucydides gives a terrible picture of
the condition of Greece in the last years under what he
calls "that rough schoolmaster war." There were "ex-
cesses of savagery" and "monstrous retaliation." "People dared the most awful deeds at a moment's caprice."
Every citizen mistrusted every other; every man feared

and hated his neighbor. The very meaning of words was changed. Moderation was despised as weakness; prudence was cowardice; recklessness and cunning were admirable. "That guilelessness which is the chief characteristic of a noble nature was laughed to scorn and disappeared."

This change from the highest to the lowest seems almost beyond belief, from the pure heroism of Marathon, from the men at Salamis advancing upon the Persians with a shout of

> Freedom —
> Freedom for country, children, wives,
> Freedom for worship, for our fathers' graves —

to a condition when, again in Thucydides' words, "every kind of depravity showed itself in Hellas." But all the other writers of the time who have come down to us confirm his account. The progress of the change as well as the extent of it can be traced in Euripides' plays, as Professor Gilbert Murray first pointed out. One of the earliest plays, the *Suppliants*, gives a wonderful picture of Athens as Pericles described her, the example of enlightenment and generosity and compassion. The chief character is Theseus, the great Athenian hero, who is approached by a band of women from Argos in behalf of their dead sons, fallen in battle against Thebes and brutally refused burial by the Thebans. They have come

for help to Athens as their only hope because, they say,
"Your city is compassionate to suffering." Theseus finally agrees to put the matter before the citizens who
alone can decide to force Thebes not to wrong the dead.
He says,

> There is no despot in our land, no man
> Who rules and makes laws at his own desire.
> Free is our city, here the people rule,
> Rich man and poor held equal by the law.

What greater proof of freedom can there be than the
herald's summons as the Assembly meets:

> "Who here will give wise counsel to the state?"
> When every man is free to speak or not,
> Each equal to the other.

The Athenians decide to champion the cause of the
helpless dead. A Theban herald who warns them not
to interfere and asks Theseus if they are strong enough to
withstand all Greece, is told

> Yes, to withstand
> All tyrants. With the good we have no quarrel.

He retorts:

> Your city takes too much upon herself,

and Theseus answers:

> Takes much and bears it; therefore she is blest.

This proud and lofty spirit shines through a few other plays, but then comes bitterness, ever increasing. Euripides is more and more losing hope for his city. In his later plays the characters are chiefly moved by violence and cruelty and vanity, fit occupants of Thucydides' Athens. "Free!" cries Hecuba in the play of that name,

> No man in the whole world is free. Not one.
> Slaves all to what they own or want or fear.

Euripides was watching the home of freedom become a place where no one could believe in freedom.

Two passages in Sophocles give the full measure of the change. In an early play the chorus sings exultingly, striking the authentic note of Athens at her height:

Wonders are there many, none more wonderful than man.
His the might that crosses seas swept white by storm blasts.
His are speech and wind-swift thought —

Just before the poet's death and the end of the war he put into words what he had come to feel as he watched the beloved city turn away from all that was good.

> Not to be born is past all prizing best.
> Next best when one has seen the light
> Is to go thither swiftly whence he came.

The glowing confidence in men's mastery of life had sunk to nothing.

Aristophanes agreed. His plays held up to the Athenians their ineptitude and their corruption and their frantic folly who, uncontrolled themselves, took it upon them to control an empire, and the theatre-goers — every Athenian went to the theatre — only laughed. They were getting in one way and another comfortable assistance from the government. What real difference did it make if officials grew rich and foreign affairs went badly?

In the *Knights*, one of Aristophanes' earlier plays, a sausage-seller enters and is greeted enthusiastically by the chorus:

	Welcome, O dearest and bravest of men.
SAUSAGE-SELLER:	I have beaten the Senate and that Cleon too. [The leading politician]
CHORUS:	Oh, tell us, dear friend.
SAUSAGE-SELLER:	I burst the door open and shouted, Good news!
	I've never known anchovies selling as cheap.
	You can get all you want for a penny.
	Then Cleon gets up — says the Spartans are here
	With an offer of peace. They won't listen.
	"With anchovies selling like that it's no time

To talk about peace. Let the fighting go
on.
It's us for the market. The meeting's dis-
solved."
Then they ran, leaping over the railings.

Enter CLEON

CLEON: I'll punish you, scoundrel. I'll have your
name down,
Inscribed on the list of the rich.
SAUSAGE-SELLER: I'll die if I don't prove that you've taken
bribes,
You robber.
CLEON: I never have robbed — except to do good
to the people.

In passage after passage in play after play Aristophanes shows up the political scene, the same in all.

There is one more witness to the city's condition.
Plato was about twenty-four when the war ended. Years
later, looking back over his life, he said, "In my youth I
cherished the hope like many another of entering upon
a political career directly I came of age. But I perceived
that the written laws and the customs were being corrupted at an astounding rate. As I gazed upon the whirlpool of public life I felt dizzy. I saw clearly as regards all
states now existing that all systems of government are
bad."

The city so judged by her greatest men was incapable of the old heroism and self-restraint which might have won out against Sparta's stern discipline. There was failure here and failure there until all resources failed and the enemy entered helpless Athens.

She fared better than a reader today would expect. In antiquity there were many instances of magnanimity from the victor to the vanquished, surprising to us with our different training. In spite of what Sparta had suffered during the long struggle of twenty-seven years she did not take vengeance on her fallen foe. She allowed Athens to be independent. Her overseas possessions were taken from her and her fleet greatly reduced, but that was all. Sparta had no thought of wrecking her or reducing her to an agricultural nation or carrying away her citizens to slave labor or installing an army of occupation. Athens was free to do as she pleased in her own country. The war had left the city untouched, but not the citizens.

The fourth century began with the realization that the fifth century's joyful confidence that men could tread the sunlit heights had ended in the conviction of men's degradation and futility. A blank hopelessness set in, and for a time a cruel tyranny took possession of the city of freedom. But Athens was still Athens. All that had made her what she was did not come to an end when the war ended. The new generation set them-

selves to the heroic task of restoring the democracy.
They put down the brutal government which had been
of Sparta's creation, and went back to the old forms.
In general they acted with a wise moderation, and prosperity returned to the city in an astonishingly short time.
But it was a different city. Outwardly it had the same
look. The war had not harmed the Acropolis; the city
was as beautiful as ever. The change was in the people.

It was shown most conspicuously in the art of the
day, as any Greek would expect. It is difficult if not
impossible for us to realize how very serious a matter
beauty and art were to the Greeks. It is related of Epami-
nondas, the greatest leader Thebes produced, that he told
the Thebans they would never be equal in war to the
Athenians unless they brought the Parthenon and the
Propylaea to Thebes. No Greek would wonder at the
remark. Of course if the Thebans lived with incomparable beauty before them they would become better
men and better fighters. Beautiful art produced beautiful
characters. That was in the Greek creed.

There is great significance, therefore, in the change
in artistic expression which began near the end of the
fifth century and went on during the entire fourth.
Briefly, it was a relaxing of control to begin with and
finally in a number of the arts a rejection of everything
that interfered with an artist's freedom. Sculpture was

least affected. Phidias would not have disowned Praxit-
eles, but in poetry and music the difference between the
new and the old was a chasm that could hardly be crossed.
Complete freedom for the artist to do whatever he
pleased was unknown in the earlier days. For instance,
strict metrical rules had governed both poetry and music,
quite as complicated and authoritative as those that
dictate the structure of the verse long beloved of English
poets, the sonnet. A genuine artist in Periclean days
would never have allowed himself, would never have
wanted, to disobey the laws of rhymic harmony. He
with all the other Athenians had drunk them in from
early boyhood when the school children began to re-
cite and listen to Homer.

There was a strong tradition of controlled art in
a people highly artistic by nature. It was thrown off by
the generation after the war apparently with complete
ease. There is a new kind of music, Aristophanes says,
which has driven out the old, and he declares that it is
rubbish, a mixture of all kinds of incongruous melodies
without rhythm or reason. The same is true of poetry.
Poets are writing about whatever comes into their heads,
"dolphins and spiders and prophets and race courses" all
jumbled together with no regard for meter or for
style. On the stage poetry had departed; only acting was
important — and the applause of the crowd. This last

was in point of fact supremely important; to capture it was the underlying motive of actor and musician and writer. Popularity was what they chiefly thought of as they tried novelty after novelty and one daring experiment followed another. The artist along with the politician had thrown aside self-discipline.

Sometime in the late fourth century Aristotle talked about art to the Athenians. He was telling them how they should educate their children. Have them learn to draw and paint, he advises, because it will train their eyes and keep them from being cheated when they buy pictures. As for music, teach them to sing and play because children have got to make a noise, but let them drop the subject early. That was the artistic level Athens had reached.

Years before Plato had said, "The only standard today is the pleasure of the hearers no matter what sort of men they are," but "those are blind who have no clear standard, and the divine is the eternal measure."

But the Greek artist now was free from standards and Greek art came to an end, never to live again.

Great teachers came forward when the fourth century was well launched. They could reach the men who thought and save them from stultifying despair. They could speak words which have rung through the world for more than two thousand years, and show men the heights men could tread. They could not touch the masses. The first who spoke to the best in fourth-century Athens belonged in actual fact to the fifth century. Socrates died soon after the war ended, but, as he told his friends in the prison on his last day, it was only his body that died. He himself, the real part of him, lived on. His death, truly heroic, was the culminating proof of the truth of what he taught and his influence after it was greater by far than before.

He had watched the state deteriorate as Thucydides and the others had, but he set himself, as they did not, to think out how it could be saved. The way he found was peculiar to himself — not by any mass movements, not by putting an end to poverty or to war or to any gross evil. He saw the salvation of the state in terms of each separate Athenian. Every man's good was the source of good for the community, just as every man's good was dependent on the good of the community. The two could not be separated. Only a good man could be a good citizen and a state could be good only when its citizens were good. The condition of the state was bound up with the condition of the souls of the men who lived in it. Socrates' eyes were fixed on the individual, and on the most individual part of him, the inner realm where alone he could be absolute master. After the great defeat of the Peloponnesian War the Athenians were proud that they had again become politically free, but Socrates saw the vulnerable life of freedom, entirely dependent as it was on men's inner freedom. He saw the danger it was in, the danger that threatened it everywhere, at all times. The very men he talked to were yielding to what must be deadly to a free state, control by the uncontrolled. Socrates told them that the citizens of a democracy could be slaves. Men were free not when freed from this or that outside rule, but when they were masters of themselves.

What he taught he lived. He was himself the example of the life of self-controlled freedom. His death was voluntary. He could have escaped if he had chosen. He chose to die.

Plato, his follower and pupil, withdrew from active life and lectured in the Academy far from the whirlpool of politics. But in his lecture room he did not turn away from it. There he said that Socrates, who never entered political life, was the true statesman. He alone had devoted himself to laying the one foundation of all good to the state, to make men turn from evil to excellence, from injustice to justice. The most excellent constitution, the best laws, were mere forms unless the people obeyed the voice of God within them. The first purpose of a government must be to train its citizens in right doing, since its strength was sapped and its very existence threatened if they became corrupt. The state must forward as a mere matter of self-preservation "the education in excellence from youth on which makes men passionately desire to become perfect citizens, knowing both how to rule and be ruled."

After Plato Aristotle took up the theme: "The state exists for the good life." "There is something within men which is divine." "There is an inborn right in the people to choose their officials because they have the capacity to judge aright in collective action."

This was high thinking, but to the great fourth-century teachers it was also clear common sense. That the prerequisite to good government was citizens who were good men seemed to them so obvious as hardly to need to be put into words, while to expect a government to be good when dishonesty had crept in among its officials, or officials to be honorable when the voters were indifferent to their being so, was a kind of folly they did not expect from Athenians.

But while they were thinking and talking, always with Athens' great past before them, a change was going on. They could not arrest or even check it. It was something fundamental and of the utmost importance, a spiritual change, which penetrated the whole state and undermined the old foundations. The earliest political manifestation of it was a demand that the Athenians should be paid for public services. This was startlingly new, but it seemed only right and reasonable. Pericles brought about pay for the jurors, which in the Athenian system meant practically every man, and pay for attendance at the Assembly followed soon after the end of the war. Both were generally approved. Plato and Aristotle strongly objected, but apparently they stood alone. Why should a man be expected to take time off from his business to decide a law-suit or a foreign policy if the state did not provide for him while he was doing so? But in Solon's day when for the first time free men came together to share in the responsibility for all, an Athenian would have thought it as strange to be paid for public service as for attending to his private business. To every one of her citizens Athens was as important as his own affairs were. She was freedom and civilization, with slavery and barbarianism continually threatening. She was the city where men "loved beauty and sought wisdom," as Pericles said. She could pre-eminently command the loyal devotion of her citizens, and devoted loyalty does not demand payment in return for service.

In the great days that followed after Salamis the spirit of Solon's Athens persisted and even grew stronger. It was the Athenians' pride and joy to give to their city. That they could get material benefits from her never entered their mind except, of course, a certain degree of safety behind her walls and her army. But the state was not an asset; they themselves were the state. There had to be a complete change of attitude before Athenians could look at the city as an employer who paid her

citizens for doing her work, and the change went deep.
Now instead of men giving to the state the state was to
give to them. What the people wanted was a government which would provide a comfortable life for them,
and with this as the foremost object ideas of freedom
and self-reliance and service to the community were
obscured to the point of disappearing. Athens was more
and more looked on as a co-operative business possessed
of great wealth in which all citizens had a right to share.
The larger and larger funds demanded made heavier and
heavier taxation necessary, but that troubled only the
well-to-do, always a minority, and no one gave a thought
to the possibility that the source might be taxed out of
existence. Politics was now closely connected with
money, quite as much as with voting. Indeed, the one
meant the other. Votes were for sale as well as officials.

The whole process was clear to Plato. Athens had
reached the point of rejecting independence, and the
freedom she now wanted was freedom from responsibility. There could be only one result. "The excess of
liberty in states or individuals," he said, "seems to pass
into excess of slavery." If men insisted on being free
from the burden of a life that was self-dependent and
also responsible for the common good, they would cease
to be free at all. Responsibility was the price every man
must pay for freedom. It was to be had on no other
terms.

Plato gave up Athens. "A lofty soul born in a mean city," he wrote, knowing that "no politician is honest, nor is there any champion of justice at whose side to fight," and that he can be of no use to the state, "holds his peace and goes his way, content if he can be pure from evil and depart in peace, with bright hopes." He does well, Plato says, and yet his good is second-rate. Only in a state he can work for, only through loyalty and patriotic devotion can a man grow to his full stature. There speaks the true Athenian, always keeping clear in his thoughts that the individual's good was the community's good, and that private life could be no more than a part of the fullness of life open to the man who could serve his country. This is Plato's farewell to the good state on earth. He turned away from freedom. He had seen the excess of it in irresponsible Athens, freedom without any counterbalancing weight of responsibility, and he wanted none of it. But by that time Athens had reached the end of freedom and was never to have it again.

Chapter III

THE SCHOOLS OF ATHENS

THE FOURTH century was an age of great prose writers and of great school teachers. Poetry had distinguished the fifth century, which had had nothing much in the way of schools. In fourth-century Athens teachers were among the most famous men of the day. They founded their own schools, Plato the Academy, Aristotle the Lyceum, Isocrates, most popular of the three, a school of rhetoric, speech-making, Plato called it disdainfully. There were a number of others, too. Athens was full of educational fervor. Such times come for the most part when there is an increasing lack of confidence in the state. If people feel that things are going from bad to worse and look at the new generation to see if they can be trusted to take charge among such dangers, they invariably conclude that they cannot and that these irresponsible young people have not been trained properly. Then the cry goes up, "What is wrong with our education?" and many answers are always forthcoming.

The great schools are a distinguishing feature of the fourth century. The fifth century took educational matters very quietly. There were primary schools for the children and a two-year military course was obligatory at the age of eighteen, but that was all there was in the way of systematic training. To the men of Periclean Athens real education began after these preliminaries. Athens became the teacher during the years of military training. The eighteen-year old Athenian, accompanied by family and friends, went to a temple and in a solemn ceremony took an oath: "I will not bring dishonor upon my weapons nor desert the comrade by my side. I will strive to hand on my fatherland greater and better than I found it. I will not consent to anyone's disobeying or destroying the constitution, but will prevent him, whether I am with others or alone. I will honor the temples and the religion my forefathers established." When he swore obedience to the constitution he knew what he was doing. Plato says, "As the children leave school the city obliges them to learn the laws."

While serving in the army, the lads were made to feel both important and responsible. Seats were reserved for them in the theatre and a prominent part given them in the many city festivals. They themselves held a show in the theatre of their exercises and drills when each was given a spear and a shield from the state. They helped garrison the many frontier posts, and inscriptions have come down to us which prove that good behavior was rewarded, sometimes even by a crown of gold. When their army life was over they had taken a long step in their education to become good citizens.

After that in the Assembly and law courts the young Athenian would learn the other lessons which made him fit for his high estate of being a guardian of Athens, to whom was entrusted the city's safety and her achievements in ways of beauty and wisdom. She was the acknowledged defender of justice and the protector of the oppressed, and she educated her citizens in excellence by her excellent laws.

But this ideal went down with many others as the war with Sparta, the Peloponnesian War, kept on for twenty-seven endless years. The new generation did not see a great and good commonweal in which they were partners together. What they saw more and more was the failure of the state and all she had stood for. They felt not only helpless, but aimless. As if in answer to this wide-spread sense of failure a host of teachers from we do not know where poured into Athens, claiming that they would give the young people what they needed. They could equip them for life. They could teach any subject that was desired, but above all they were teachers of rhetoric, of the art of persuasion which would make a man able to convince others and lead them where he wished. There was no surer road to prosperity and power.

The Sophists, the Wise Men, as they were called, had a great success for many years. They came to Athens long before the end of the War and their popularity continued until the great fourth-century teachers started their schools. The accusation most often made against them was that they took money for their teaching. This aroused Athens' wonder and contempt. To impart wisdom only when you were paid proved that you had no right of entry into the noble company of the wise. Plato charged his pupils nothing; Isocrates charged only foreigners. Athens was still far from being what a visiting prince called Rome just before Cicero's day, "City where everything is for sale."

Aristotle did not found the Lyceum until some years after Plato's death, so that for the first half of the century there were only two great rival schools. The Academy's aim was to prepare men for philosophy with a dim and yet exciting possibility of producing or discovering among them a supremely good and great philosopher-ruler who would inaugurate the good state. Isocrates' school claimed to be a preparation for life and the purely intellectual was ruled out, except for mathematics, which he grudgingly conceded was good mental exercise, "a gymnastic of the mind" he called it. But that was his only concession in such ways. His school was practical, he said, designed to turn out young men fitted to play their part in the city's life.

Between Plato at the head of one theory of education and Isocrates at the head of the other, Athens had not an easy choice. Each school had ardent champions and the hot disputes were materially heightened by the two headmasters taking an active part in them. Isocrates attacked the very foundation of the Academy, declaring that Plato's idea of philosophy was fundamentally false. "Never," he said, "does that deserve the name of philosophy (the love of wisdom) which is of no immediate use." He was himself, he claimed, a true philosopher, clear-headed, realistic, sensible. "I hold that man wise who can usually think out the best course to take and that man a philosopher who seeks to gain that insight." A mere theorizer, he said, was incapable of it, a man of finespun speculations and lifeless abstractions.

He never mentioned his great rival by name, but here and there in his speeches, pamphlets rather, for although he taught oratory he was no orator and preferred writing to speaking, he dropped remarks about idealists who "busy themselves with impracticable plans" for the very practical matter of politics and "prefer to chatter empty nonsense rather than further some attainable good." He saw the relation of his thought to Plato's as that of the far-seeing statesman to the high-flying visionary. He was bent on a sweeping reform of political life which would result in bringing back the old personal independence and devotion to the state. Plato was bent upon the same thing, but to him the only way to benefit the state was for each Athenian to take a course which would benefit his own soul. One can see Isocrates' humorous shrug as he dismissed such foolishness.

Plato struck back and with harder blows. He held rhetoric in contempt and described the teachers of it as "Hunters after young men of wealth and position with sham education as their bait and a fee for their object." He dismissed as peremptorily their subject matter, Isocrates' "art of composing and delivering speeches" which he was so proud to teach. Plato says caustically in one of those comments of his which fling open a door and disclose a height not seen before, "Nothing spoken or written is of any great value if the object is merely to be believed, not to be criticised and thus learn more." The only writing that really brings profit is "engraving on men's souls justice and goodness and nobility." Sometimes he disguised his attack under an appearance of speaking jestingly, but the disguise was thin. He described "philosopher-politicians (a malicious phrase that hit Isocrates off to the life) who aim at being both and end by being neither." "But," he added kindly, "every man ought to be esteemed who pursues anything in the slightest degree like wisdom. Still, we shall do well to see them as they really are." It was a commendation nicely calculated to arouse Isocrates' fury.

Both headmasters had admirable platforms. Plato's was brief, but comprehensive: "Education is the fairest thing that the best of men can have," and "The particular learning which leads you throughout your life to hate what should be hated and love what should be loved will be rightly called education. People are educated who have seen the beautiful and just and good in their truth."

Isocrates' declaration was on another level, a list of attainable qualities, but there could hardly be a better description of a gentleman. He said that a man he educated would be "First, capable of usually hitting upon the right course. Secondly, he will meet any company, however disagreeable, with easy good-temper and show to all men fairness and gentleness. Thirdly, he will be master of himself in misfortune and pain. Fourthly and most important, his head will not be turned by success. Those whose soul is well tuned to play its part in all these ways I regard as educated."

Whatever was wrong in Athens of the fourth century it was not the conception of what ought to be the aim of education or the standards for an educated man.

Just what went on in the schools we do not know. No description of the courses has come down to us or the methods of teaching or the arrangements for work. The nearest we can come to the day-by-day training is a brief parody of the Academy by a comic writer. It is a dialogue with something of an Aristophanic flavor.

FIRST SPEAKER: "What about Plato? What's being investigated there?"

SECOND SPEAKER: "Well, in the gymnasium of the Academy I saw a lot of lads drawing up definitions of natural objects; at that moment it was a cucumber. First they dropped their heads and thought a long, long time. Then suddenly one spoke up and said it was a circular vegetable, another declared it was an herb, a third suggested a tree. But Plato very gently and without losing his temper told them to try again. So they all went back to the beginning."

This is an instructive little passage, parody though it is. It shows to begin with that a school for boys was part of the Academy and also that they were trained in something besides the traditional logic and mathematics. Cucumber apart, Plato was trying to make his pupils observe. He was not giving them information or making them learn by heart; they were finding things out for themselves. Moreover the cucumber points clearly and surprisingly to his having antedated Aristotle who is always said to have been the first to have his students observe actual facts in the real world.

Apparently a stiff entrance examination guarded the Academy proper, and when that was passed the young men faced a number of years of hard work, chiefly in logic and mathematics, with a distant prospect of sometime being fit to approach divine philosophy. It seems a program for the very few, but the Academy was eminently successful. After all, it was in Athens.

Isocrates was still more popular. He says himself that he had "more pupils than all the schools of philosophy put together." The training he offered, although not on Plato's austere heights, was excellent. The lads were required to compose speeches on great and noble subjects which, he said, would elevate and liberate their minds, turning their attention to lofty causes and making them acquainted with lives of high endeavor. Such a discipline, Isocrates believed, formed their taste and freed them from the bondage of the commonplace.

When Aristotle founded the Lyceum both Plato and Isocrates were dead. The Academy, it is true, was still important, but it must certainly have lost out with Plato's death and it had to give place to the new school. The Lyceum was new in every sense. Its object was not to arouse the love of the good and develop the search for it, but to train and inform the mind. Apparently the Academy had convinced Aristotle that no school or institution could do the first; the second could be done in a classroom. The knowledge Plato would lead his young Academicians to was the vision of the truth. Aristotle wanted for his pupils accurate knowledge of facts and some understanding of their relations to each other. We know little more about the school, but from Aristotle's writings the subjects offered seem to have been encyclopedic, comprising such degrees of difference as the principles of dramatic criticism and the reproduction of the eel. We hear of a large library, certainly an innovation over the Academy (Plato did not like books), and of maps on the walls, the first mention of them. Also we are told that Aristotle turned the practical management over to the students, appointing one lad head for ten days and then another, saving himself, no doubt, an infinity of trouble. There were other lecturers besides himself. He gave two courses of lectures, one to advanced students and one to any who chose to attend.

A large part of his writings that have come down to us are lectures and notes for lectures. They are almost entirely bare unadorned outlines of thought. He did not care to be a writer. What he could have done in that way a few beautiful passages show, but he wanted to be a teacher and for a thousand years or more he was the supreme teacher.

It is our great loss that we know so little of what was taught in the schools and how, but the most important matter we do know, what their headmasters were like. We can conclude with security that there has never been a generation better educated than the one that ushered in the end of Athens.

Chapter IV

THE SCHOOL TEACHERS

Isocrates

THE CONTEMPORARY writer who has left the clearest picture of the age — except for the comedian, Menander — is Isocrates, the admired and popular teacher, Plato's rival. He lived to be a very old man and gave up school-teaching, but he never gave up trying to teach the Athenian people. He was not a practical politician, but even more than a teacher he was a statesman, and in the great sense of the word, a man of extraordinary insight and foresight. Athens had need of such a guide, but she had reached a point where she could not make use of him.

After the end of the great war, thanks to Sparta's merciful use of her victory, the spirit of the Athenians was quickly rekindled and the democracy re-established. It proved eminently successful in dealing with the acute problems that faced the city: a sea-power deprived of almost all her fleet; a country increasing in population beyond her boundaries, deprived of her colonies. In an astonishingly short time Athens regained her old position of mistress of the sea and the way to new colonies lay open. The people were emphatically in power. The Assembly which alone could declare war or make a treaty or pass a law was in the hands of the majority who paid little regard to the cultured minority. Nevertheless, life in Athens was safe and well-ordered. Of course men used their right of free speech, most precious possession to Athenians, to criticize everything the government did or left undone. Isocrates says, "We all sit around complaining that we have never been worse governed, while showing by our actions that we like our brand of democracy better than that of our forefathers," and the truth seems to be that people in general were more comfortable than they had ever been.

But Isocrates was too far-sighted to be at ease. Foreign affairs, always the weak point in a democracy, were not going well and the reason, he told the Athenians, was to be found at home. They were thinking, he said, not of their duties as citizens, but of their rights. They were looking to the state to guarantee not freedom as in the old days, but privilege. Great danger lay in that course. Men bent on self-interest were always shortsighted. They could rise to long views, to where they could see the good of the whole country, only when they looked beyond their own affairs, and the state in which men did not do that was doomed. "You have no breadth of view," he told the Athenians. "You do not give equal attention to the men who address you, but really listen only to those who support your desires. If you truly wished to find out what is best for the country you would listen more to those who oppose you than to those who try to please you. How can men decide wisely without giving an unbiased hearing to both sides? But you — you think those better friends of the people who dole out money to them than those who serve the state disinterestedly." And yet the welfare of the state was absolutely essential to the welfare of the citizens. "But the masses," Isocrates said, "like better a person who flatters them than one who really benefits them. They would actually rather lose out with a man who smiles at everybody than profit with a man who is aloof. If they like some one they will forgive all faults and mistakes."

The men who smiled at them and won their votes were not statesmen equal to their task. They could take from the rich to give to the poor; they could stimulate trade; they could see to it that every Athenian had a free ticket to the theatre. Affairs at home gave them little trouble, but affairs abroad were another story. In point of fact, the foreign policy they were pursuing could not but end disastrously. They were trying with no success to appease Persia, still the great Oriental power, while fighting Greeks in one exhausting war after another and turning allies into enemies. Athens was being isolated at the very time when the Eastern menace had drawn nearer than ever before. Early in the fourth century Persia took over the Greek cities in Asia Minor with the consent of the other Greeks. Sparta had fought her and been beaten and there was no other Greek state able to go on with the war. Xenophon quotes from the treaty which he calls The King's Peace (The King at that time meant the Persian ruler.): "The King thinks it just that the cities in Asia shall belong to him. Should any parties refuse to accept this peace I will make war upon them by land as well as by sea, with ships and with money."

Greeks in the past had sometimes made use of Persian help in their wars against each other. Athens herself had done so. But never before had Greeks given up Greeks to become slaves to a despot. The step was not only deeply humiliating, it was full of danger. Persia was now on the Mediterranean, next-door neighbor to Athens.

Isocrates was the only man in the city who spoke out clearly about what was happening. He denounced the treaty. It was correctly called "the King's Peace," he said, for it had turned out to the advantage of the Persians alone. "We should not allow an agreement which has given allies of our own up to the enemy, to stand for a single day. We may rightly blame our envoys because they made a treaty in the interest of the

barbarian — they acted toward him as if we had gone
to war for his sake."

It may well be that Isocrates alone saw the danger.
The greatest minds in Athens had turned away from
politics. Plato at the Academy, withdrawn from active
life, was planning his ideal republic; Aristotle was his
pupil; the Athenian state got no help from either. Demosthenes and a host of brilliant speakers were busy
pleading in the law courts. Isocrates seems to have been
the only one who opposed the treaty, and certainly he
was the only one who looked at it in relation to all
Greece.

Some sense of Greek unity had begun to develop,
but very inadequately. Greece was not destined to go
that way. But Isocrates was its ardent advocate. He
saw it as the one condition upon which Greece, and
so Athens, could keep freedom and independence. This
was not only an unusual point of view, it was unique.
He alone of all the great men of his day passed the
boundaries of the little city-state to embrace the whole
country. His cherished dream was a United Greece,
which years later Aristotle said would be able, if brought
about, to rule the world. Isocrates had no thought of
that, but only of saving his city and therefore the country of which she was the heart.

The passion of his life was Athens. To read him is
to be carried constantly back to the glorious past when

Pericles said of the Athenians: "Their bodies they devote to their country as though they were not their own; their true self is their mind, which is most truly their own when employed in her service." Isocrates loved Athens like that. He saw her as the place where civilization had first come to birth, the moderation and gentleness and self-control without which there is no civilization. Athens had become what Pericles had called her, "The School of Hellas," where, Isocrates said, lessons could be learned so lofty and so true they could benefit not only Greece, but the world. The Athenian constitution based on free men willingly serving the state was, he never wearied of saying, the true expression of the Athenian character. The Founding Fathers of Democracy had been merely spokesmen for the people. They had established only what the Athenians themselves wanted. "The constitution is the soul of the state," Isocrates said.

Feeling thus he watched the encroaching power of Persia, barbarianism approaching to blot out civilization, slavery to put an end to freedom. He saw the Greek world, the only place where men could be free, worn down by perpetual quarrels, Greeks forever fighting Greeks in petty wars which left both sides exhausted. There could be only one end, the West so weakened that it would fall before the East. In a pamphlet full of passionate feeling he wrote: "As for that barbaric power, nothing is more to his purpose than to prevent us from ever ceasing to quarrel with each other, whereas we are so far from fomenting rebellion among his subjects that when by some good fortune it breaks out we have actually helped him to put it down. We have conceded Asia to him and Greek cities. He has rightly conceived an utter contempt for us. Our own folly is responsible, not his power. Most of the population in Persia has been trained for servitude more effectively than the slaves in our country. Even those in highest office have never governed their lives by a regard for justice or the common interest. They are all subject to one man's power and they keep their souls in a state of abject and cringing fear."

Could such a country defeat freedom and high civilization and drive them from the world? That is the question Isocrates faced. An oriental despotism with only slaves for subjects could — she had already proved it — defeat separate Greek states, but she surely could be no match for a United Greece, free men acting as one nation to defend the whole country. Was union possible? What had always happened in the past was that the moment Persia relaxed, Greeks fell to fighting each other. Sometimes they even preferred to submit to her rather than to a neighbor grown too powerful. And yet only a hundred years ago at Marathon, at Salamis, they had united and grandly succeeded. Might not history be repeated when the same danger threatened? So Isocrates meditated, seeing as even Aristotle years later was unable to see, that the day of the small independent state was passing, if it had not already passed, and searching for some endurable substitute which would save for the world what was best in it, of which the core was Athens.

His solution was a union of Greeks brought about by an invasion of Persia which if successful, as Isocrates took for granted, would not only save freedom and civilization in Greece, but extend them into Asia. He threw himself into urging this course with all his power. The idea of a united Greece possessed him, but how he detested war, how he hated to champion a war even in the cause of Greek union, is clear to see in a pamphlet he published at this time. He told the Athenians that they should join the other Greeks quite as much to spread the blessings they enjoyed as to preserve them, fight Persia, but in such a way that the war would be marked out from all other wars, "More like a sacred mission than a military expedition," a mission to bring freedom to those in the dark prison of slavery. Greece could show Persia how to be free. Then, Isocrates said, whether a man lived in the East or the West would not matter. Excellence and wisdom have no national boundaries. "The man who shares our highest thoughts," he told the

Athenians, "is a Greek in a truer sense that he who shares merely our blood."

This is true internationalism enunciated twenty years before Alexander the Great declared his intention of uniting the East and the West and at a time when every state, big or little, was the passive and often the active enemy of all the others. Plato, who had his own brand of internationalism, said that the only profitable basis for intercourse between men was friendship. On this point the two rival school teachers could in some sort meet.

Isocrates' crusade was preached in vain. The Athenians were not interested in war as a moral force, whether to make democracy safe, or to end all wars, or to do any widespread glorious good. They were willing of course to fight to defend their country, also to acquire a useful colony, but that was all. Persia was across the sea. She could be ignored, for the present certainly. In the rest of Greece Isocrates' failure was even more complete. The Greeks would not unite no matter what danger threatened from the East. They would not give up their centuries-old feuds and their dislike of each other's ways. As for Persia, she was undoubtedly moving westward, but it was always possible that she would be content with what she already had, and it was not possible that Sparta, for instance, would come to terms with Messenia and allow her to have a voice in anything that mattered to Spartans. That particular dream of a great united Greece carrying out a sacred martial mission Isocrates had to dismiss.

When he preached his crusade he was almost sixty years old, but he lived to be nearly a hundred, and forty years of life still lay before him, years of increasing discouragement. He believed in democracy as the other intellectuals of the day did not, which is to say that he believed in the Athenian people, but he was completely aware both of the danger in unchecked majority rule perpetually threatening to pass over into mob-rule, and of the fact that while the best in a community must be a minority, rule by a minority had again and again resulted in loss of freedom, the greatest loss of all. Was it possible for the majority to become wise rulers of the state? That was the question which preoccupied him during the last years of his life when his faith in what the people would — or could — do grew less and less confident.

The picture of the late fourth-century Athenians he has left us shows his deep discouragement with them which yet never lessens his devotion to Athens. Once the citizens were "men schooled when young to be industrious and frugal," "accustomed in their early days never to regard public office as a chance for private gain," who "considered poverty among their fellow-citizens as their own disgrace," and "measured their well-being not by being able to outdo each other, but by the soberness of their daily life and the absence of want among the whole people," the only standards, Isocrates comments caustically, which are not vulgar. But wise and right though these had been proved to be, they had all been discarded. Now "young men no longer trained to hardihood are wasting their youth in soft living"; "lawlessness is looked upon as liberty, license as happiness." "The state has become a means to satisfy selfish desires."

This is not the sour criticism of discontented old age. It is a judgment passed upon the Athenians by one who loved them. He saw at last that they were not capable of looking beyond their little state. Greek union, military mission to Persia, the one was as impossible to them as the other. Yet to keep on appeasing Persia and turning allies into enemies was, inevitably, ruin. Must he give up Athens? That was unthinkable. In his anguish of mind he began to think thoughts about war, what it had brought to the world. He had read Thucydides. He was familiar with the picture the great historian had drawn of how the morality of the individual Athenian and of the state had crumbled away during the war with Sparta. "War is a rough teacher," Thucydides wrote, "and fits men's characters to their condition." He told his readers why wars were fought, "Because of the desire for power which greed and ambition inspire." Every schoolboy in fourth-century Athens knew that the end of twenty-seven years of bitter fighting was that Sparta conquered only to have all that she had gained taken from her speedily by Persia. That lesson of what war accomplishes Isocrates had learned.

Thucydides had thought the lesson never would be learned. "The kind of events that once took place," he wrote, "will by reason of human nature take place again." He saw the scroll of history unrolling forever stained with blood. Isocrates would not admit this as a possibility, not for Athens. "You can renounce war," he told the Athenians. "It is war which has in every way overwhelmed us with misfortune. If we live at peace with the rest of the world we shall live in security and advance in prosperity. The condition for peace is not money by which men can be bought, nor force by which men can be compelled. It is the all-conquering power of good will. The Athenian spirit is the best, the loftiest. Other nations feel it to be such. They want to be our friends. That is our surest defense, better by far than a powerful navy."

"I know that it is dangerous to oppose you," he said, "and that although this is a free government there is no real freedom of speech, but none the less I am going to speak out. I tell you we should make peace with all mankind and stop setting our hearts upon ruling the sea. Once, we recognized that it is not just for the stronger to rule over the weaker, as indeed we still recognize it in private life. But apart from that I say that such power is not to the advantage of the state. It depraves all who have it and all who seek it. They are led on until they even lay waste the land of those they conquer and rob them of a part of it, even disperse them from their homes."

In the case of individuals, he said, such actions would be abhorrent to all, but the state has been held not to be bound by the ideas of personal morality. "Wise self-control in a man is praised," he said, "but not in a state. Yet it is far more important for a state than for an individual to follow the good." Athens' glory is that she is a democracy, "but a rich and powerful democracy cannot endure." True democracy "is the renunciation of the struggle for power. Treat weak states as you wish stronger to treat you. . . . The only sure foundation for a nation's prosperity is a religious regard for the rights of others. . . . But first you must be persuaded that minding your own business is better than meddling with other people's."

Needless to say the Athenian politicians were not converted to a programme of peace. Isocrates' pamphlet was no doubt widely read — he was very popular — and with no more practical effect than it would have had in any other place in any other period of history. But what is remarkable is that it did him very little harm. Yet

Athenians took Athens' supremacy at sea as much for granted as Englishmen took Great Britain's, and it is easy to imagine what would have been the fate of any man in Victorian or Edwardian England, any politician, preacher, writer, who urged renouncing war, giving up the command of the sea and living in peace with all men. He would have been so denounced, ridiculed, despised, that he would never again have found an audience. Not so Isocrates in Athens. He went through periods of unpopularity, of course, but they were always brief, and he died honored and revered.

Many years after the pamphlet on peace came out he wrote Philip of Macedon urging him to join the Greeks with him in the attack he was planning on Persia. By that time Isocrates saw no other hope for his city. He could no longer think of the best for her, only the best possible. She would not take the way of peace and her wars had almost drained away her strength. In those years the world around him had changed. Macedon, a country on the northern boundary of Greece, and herself partly Greek, had come forward as an important power. Her king, Philip, was a great general and a great statesman who was always intervening in Greek quarrels and showing that the side he was on came off best. It did not need Isocrates' keen vision to discern that there was here a possible rival power to Persia and a growing threat to Greek freedom, but to him the danger from

Macedon was beyond all comparison the lesser evil. Persia was a barbarian outside of the civilized world; the Macedonians were indeed very little Greek and by no means really civilized, but they were not out-and-out barbarians. Philip had been educated in Greece and had declared himself an admirer of Athens. It was more than possible that whatever he did to the rest of Greece he would leave Athens free. But again Isocrates' hopes came to nothing. What chance could pamphlets, however well reasoned, have against the fiery eloquence of Philip's arch-enemy, Demosthenes? The old man lived just long enough to see the Greeks under Demosthenes' leadership suffer a crushing defeat, outgeneraled and outfought by Philip.

In the appeal to Philip to lead the Greek armies against Persia Isocrates was not reversing himself on the matter of war and peace. He saw the expedition as one of defense, not attack, in view of Persia's threatening position on the Mediterranean, and a war to defend one's country was in another category, it was good and glorious. Isocrates could advocate it unhesitatingly and the letter to Philip is one of his noblest pieces of writing. Yet shortly before his death he wrote: "I am not able because of my age to speak out all that I grasp in my thought, but I do say that it is a noble undertaking in the midst of the madness and evil of the world to be able to keep to sanity, to cease from war and detest power, knowing the disasters that come from them." He had returned to his conviction that war was the great evil and peace the great good for the world.

His claim to fame does not rest on his political sagacity. Historians have not yet decided between him and Demosthenes. In any event, the most forward-looking foresight seems shortsighted when considered after a lapse of centuries. But the fact that he was the first to declare (under Thucydides' guidance) that power tends to corrupt and absolute power corrupts absolutely, and the first to urge giving up war as a policy and substituting good will for armed forces, sets him so far in advance of his age that on that score alone he could never be forgotten. These two great ideas express in a sense what he was. No small views or selfish views had a place in his mind. He was built on large and noble lines. Whatever he urged was for some high good. He was not always right, certainly as we see matters, but he was always disinterested, always a great patriot, throughout his life putting his country first.

History, which does not concern itself with impracticable ideals or, at the least, ideals never put into practice, has very generally passed him over. Caesar was never disturbed by the baseless fabric of visions, and his ideas of war and of the best way to conquer are known everywhere. But narrow and limited ideas, however long their life, have a narrow and limited sphere of influence and must sometime give way to more width and breadth of thought. Perhaps the lonely Greek thinker who could not consider war as the Roman did, only in terms of one nation conquering another, but must see it in relation to all human activities as helping or harming mankind, may prove in the end to have a longer life. This at least is certain, that what Caesar thought is not of importance today, but Isocrates had thoughts which apply as much to us as to his Athens.

Plato

When Plato gave up politics and turned to teaching he was not in his own eyes withdrawing from the service of the state. To him that would have been a betrayal of the best. He says, "The greatest and fairest sort of wisdom by far is that which is concerned with the ordering of states." He founded his school with the aim of giving Athens a new order, of providing her with what she most needed, wise and good political leaders. During his short essay into politics what had impressed him most profoundly and most painfully was the low stature morally and intellectually of the leading politicians. They were all of them striving for their own selfish interests and the average decent citizen was incapable of standing out against them. Plato had found himself powerless, and he left the political scene with the conviction that the one essential was good leaders. To find young men capable of leading and to develop to the full their capacity by the right kind of education was now his object. The Academy might save Athens.

At heart Plato was a reformer, not the philosophical contemplative men called him. A life of contemplation was far from what he wanted for his pupils, but they must go through a long period of preparation. They were being trained for a sternly practical task, but it was the most important and the most difficult of all the tasks men engage in, building up a good state, leading people to understand the good and so desire to bring it about. For such an enterprise the preparation must be long and difficult. Necessarily the ordinary man would misjudge it. He would see a school for political education completely withdrawn from practical politics, even in its situation, a quiet hilltop outside the city; the students living a retired life absorbed in studies which had no remote connection with anything political. When he met any of them they would seem to him tongue-tied and awkward or just plain stupid, anything but well-trained, precisely the opposite to a keen politician. Plato, of course, was serenely aware of all this. In one of his dialogues he describes the students, or rather he makes a kind of tender fun of them. They do not even know, he says, their way about the city, where the market-place is or the Assembly, much less what laws are being passed, and least of all what people are talking about. And they are quite unconscious of their ignorance because only their bodies are there; their minds are far away. They have left behind them the commonplaces of thought and talk; they are trying to find truth. But, mark well, this is the true preparation for the political life because only if a man has knowledge of what is true and good can he lead men to bring about a good state, to change injustice into justice, to put self-control in the place of outside control. Only he can bring order and peace to a state who has within himself the calm and the harmony which are God's.

The plan for the Academy was founded on this basic truth, Plato declared, and therefore it was practicable; it could be carried out. "Until philosophers are kings or the kings and princes of this world have the spirit and power of philosophy, and political greatness and wisdom meet in one, and those commoner natures who pursue either to the exclusion of the other are compelled to stand aside, cities will never have rest from their evils, no, nor the human race. That either of these alternatives is impossible, or both, I see no reason to suppose. That in the course of the ages there will not be one such, who would venture to affirm? But one is enough to bring into existence the ideal." That one exemplar who would show the world how it could have rest from its evils might be produced by the Academy. If that happened it would indeed have fulfilled its object.

This was the idea that shaped the school. Young men, older men, too, would have a place where they could develop to the full whatever capacity they had of seeking and finding the truth.

One wonders what Socrates would have made of it all. He had been dead eleven years when the Academy was started. If Plato ever in imagination placed the beloved master in those remote and quiet halls, among those earnest seekers after knowledge of the highest, he must have realized how far from Socrates he had come. Knowing Socrates as he did, he could not have failed to see him casting a humorous and skeptical look — but a very kindly one — at both Academy and Academicians.

Socrates too had sought for the knowledge of the highest, but the place where he looked for it was not remote and consecrated to the higher pursuits. It was a gymnasium where he would settle down to talk to a man or two resting from exercise, or a street corner where someone came up to pass the time of day with him, or a supper party where men drank good wine and talked freely. He lived his life like that, always with people. Cicero said of him that he brought philosophy down from heaven into the cities and homes of men, just what the eager young Academicians strictly avoided. Socrates never conceived, any more than Christ did, of establishing an institution to spread the truth — an

Academy or a theological seminary. To both, the truth
they knew could not be expressed in statements and
taught to others. A man could be aroused to seek it, that
was all. He could find it only by seeking it himself. Socrates never wrote down a word; Christ wrote only once,
with his finger in the dust.

Plato too believed that only those who sought could
find. His fundamental conviction was one with Socrates':
There was in every man a spark of good, of the divine,
which could be kindled into a flame. As St. John, the
Greek thinker among the Evangelists, was to say centuries later, "The true light which lighteth every man
that cometh into the world." To make the spark blaze up
in the souls of men was the object of Socrates' work,
which he called the service of God, and it was no less
Plato's. The Academy was designed for the service of
God just as much as Socrates' talks on the street corner.
Nevertheless, when all is said and done, it is impossible
to place Socrates in the Academy, and Plato lived there
for forty years. To him it was the place where young
men capable of seeking the truth could pursue their
search uninterrupted and with a single mind. Plato was
forty years old when he founded it, but he still had his
dreams.

He himself would have rejected utterly the idea that
he ever dreamed. He considered himself first of all a
practical man with a practical aim in view, good govern-

ment, a good life for men. He never thought of himself as a philosopher in our sense of the word, nor yet as the discoverer of the Ideas, and methods of making discoveries in the realm of the ideal. It is odd, but true, that he disliked finespun theorizing and far-flung flights of thought which have been so indissolubly united with him through the ages that the word Platonic carries with it a notion of unreality. Plato was bent on exactly the opposite, on finding what was of value for life. He was convinced that truth was supremely fruitful of good to men. The conviction that truth when found necessarily results in definite, positive good was the cornerstone of the Platonic philosophy in the eyes of its founder. Other philosophers tried to find the truth to rest in it when they were intellectually satisfied. What they wanted was an explanation and when they had got it they were not concerned with the results it might have for good or ill. That consideration was outside of their philosophical interest as they conceived it. To Plato this would have had no sense. Truth was to be sought precisely because it always had good results. Aristotle wanted to know. He prized knowledge for its own sake. Plato wanted only the knowledge that would — must — work out into right action because it alone was true knowledge. Truth was always creative of goodness. The Greeks and notably the Athenians were pre-eminently practical. What was good must do good. When Christ said, "Ye shall know them by their fruits," he expressed a fundamental Greek conviction. If the fruit was good it was unnecessary to examine the root.

They carried this idea through everything. Aristophanes said that poetry was to be admired only if it made men better and that the supreme poets were those who "guided the city to the truth." Plato agreed. Good art could not fail to be an influence for the good life. "In the art of the painter," he writes, "and every other creative art, ugliness and discord are nearly allied to evil just as grace and harmony are to excellence. Those who grow up amid images of moral deformity silently gather a festering mass of corruption in their own souls. Let our artists be those who are gifted to discern the true nature of the beautiful. Then will our youth dwell in a land of health amid fair sights and sounds; and beauty shall flow into eyes and ears like a health-giving breeze from a purer region." "I do believe," he says, "that an involuntary homicide is less criminal than to be a deceiver about beauty or goodness."

That a work of art could be ugly would have been to a Greek a contradiction in terms. That that could be art which presented only or chiefly the abnormal would have seemed nonsense to the most artistic race in history. When Plato said that to describe the ugliness and evil of men was to express only the appearance, not the truth, he was speaking for Greece. Homer, the Greek

Bible, stated what was basic to the Greek view of life when he said, "The divine for which all men long."

But to ignore the bad was not Plato's way. He was not a romanticist. To the medieval world he was the great realist who showed men what was truly real. He had indeed his own notion of what reality was, but he can never be charged with looking away from what was unpleasant or seeing good in evil or harmony in discord. The ugly was there. It was what the vast majority saw, but the seeker for the truth, the artist, the philosopher, saw something else. They could discern the meaning, what was significant and what was unimportant. That way lay the truth, which could be found only by seeing through the appearance. "One must turn the eye," Plato said, "from the perishing world to what is real and eternal...turn the eye of the soul to the light." Yet Plato's preoccupation was always with the perishing world. "Looking at the good in all its purity a man can use it as a pattern."

Through all the years of his peaceful academic retirement he held fast to the conviction that the aim of the good life was to forward the good of the state. This sharply practical side of him has been little emphasized, but he illustrated it in his life up to the end. He would always leave the Academy if he thought he could be of use, and take part in some political venture. We know of three such occasions, the last when he was a very old

man, when he went to Sicily and risked his life trying
to convert an irresponsible tyrant. He wrote that if he
had refused, "I feared to see myself at last nothing but
words — a man who would never willingly lay hand to
any concrete task."

The Academy did not save Athens. It had a long
life, longer than any school there has ever been. When
it was closed it had been in existence for nearly nine
hundred years, but as far as our scanty knowledge goes
it had no effect politically. No great and good leaders
came from it, no philosopher-king to banish injustice
and establish good government on earth. We do not
know even of one who tried to do so. In politics the
Academy was a failure and that fact would have condemned it in Plato's eyes.

No institution was ever started with a loftier purpose or a better reason to hope for success. The founder
has held his own for more than two thousand years in
the very first rank of the good and the great, and the
best part of his life was spent there working for it. And
yet a few years after he died it proved powerless to
give any help to Athens in her extremity. During all the
crucial Macedonian contest after the death of Alexander the Great, nothing was heard of it and from that
time on history does not take it into account. It dropped
out of its pages and never figured in them again. We have
too little information about it to know why it sank into

the background and remained there. Plato's faith, however, his intensity of conviction that those who seek the
truth find it and that there is nothing else worth seeking,
broke through the Academy's walls and for two thousand years it has influenced profoundly the course of
thought in the western world. But to Plato, who had
put the great effort of his life into the Academy, it became increasingly evident that the school was failing. It
was never designed to enshrine and develop a set of
truths Plato believed which Academicians would accept.
Such a conception was as far from Plato as from Socrates.
Truth could be found. That glorious possibility he kept
before each student, but only through a search which
must be lonely and hard and might be long. As time
went on he discovered how few were willing to make
the effort, and disappointment after disappointment
came to him.

Glimpses of them are given here and there in his
letters and they are of great interest because they are
a record, however slight, of what he himself felt and
they are the only personal references we have. Sometimes briefly he himself emerges and we see for a moment
what he suffered in the Academy. Over and over again
he emphasizes the necessity of hard work and the extreme difficulty of getting the young to do it. Nothing
can be accomplished without it, but only a few are willing to make the struggle although there are many who

are eager to make the start. "I know without being told," he writes, "that no one need be surprised if a young man on hearing of a really great enterprise yields to the spell of the ideal life." Young men in numbers had come to the Academy full of eagerness to learn lofty truths. "To such," the letter goes on to say, "one must point out how much hard work is necessary." From the Dialogues we know that instead of starting in at once on elevated discussions about the nature of the Good these ardent young people were set toilsome tasks in mathematics and logic with almost invariably the same discouraging result.

Some persevered. "If a man genuinely wishes to learn," another letter says, "he sees in the course marked out for him a path of enchantment which he must strain every nerve to follow or die in the attempt. When this conviction has taken possession of him he never ceases to practice such habits as will make him an intelligent student able to reason soberly by himself." But these are the very few. "The others as soon as they see how much there is to study, how much hard work is involved, decide the plan is too difficult for them." In those years of teaching Plato had seen so many fall by the way, often those who were greatly endowed, qualified to enter the race for the best prize life can give, the knowledge of the truth, raising high his hopes for them. "The self-indulgent," he writes, "and those incapable of hard work persuade themselves that they know enough; they have no need to learn more." Others of a still poorer quality "are contemptuous in a thoroughly offensive manner" of what they cannot learn easily. Some even do not know that they have failed and "feel loftily that they have acquired awesome learning."

Plato's disappointments are listed there, and as an old man he concludes in one of the last letters: "I do not think the attempt to teach everyone the subjects to which I devote myself is a good thing; only the few are capable of finding the truth for themselves with a little guidance." The words are calm and resolute, but they express the failure of hopes cherished for forty years.

Pindar had said a hundred years before, that a man could be truly great only "through inborn glory; he who learns from teaching is a twilight man." Plato had hoped that the man who was born glorious could be discovered, could find himself, in the school, and go forward to the greatest goal. And yet the one pupil he had who was most unmistakably possessed both of inborn glory and the driving power of hard work, must have brought him the keenest disappointment of all. For the last twenty years of his life Aristotle was his pupil. As Socrates fanned the spark in Plato so Plato did in Aristotle.

The flame in the younger man, however, gave forth a different light, and it is impossible that both men, being such as they were, did not recognize this. The scientist's love of learning and of assembling and ordering all his eyes and ears brought to him, which burned in Aristotle, was not shared by Plato. To him the truth was not to be found in that way. Aristotle did not leave the Academy until Plato died, twenty years after he had entered it. There seems to have been no question of Aristotle's succeeding his master. A man immeasurably his inferior got the post. It is true that by then Aristotle had begun to disagree with Plato, and it may be that he wanted to be free of the Academy, but there had certainly been no real break between the two men, for soon after Plato's death Aristotle paid him a tribute which showed tender affection as well as deep admiration. He wrote:

He alone and first of men showed plain for all to see
By the life he lived, by all the words he ever spoke to men,
That the good man is the happy man, now, here,
    upon the earth.

What Plato thought about him is far from clear. He never in any of his writings mentioned his name. Still, the astonishing fact that when it came to choosing a new head Aristotle was passed over certainly suggests that on Plato's side there had been a withdrawal if not an actual break. Unquestionably during the years of their close connection he had learned what this pupil of his was, delighted in the brilliancy and power of that young unfolding mind and felt a growing hope that here might be the supreme philosopher for whose production first of all the Academy had been designed. The regret that finally came when he realized that the man so greatly gifted beyond all others would never — could never — receive and carry forward his own torch, must have been the culminating disappointment in those forty years of unfulfilled hopes.

And yet what Aristotle remembered most of all was that Plato was happy. Aristotle had watched him to the end, an old man whose dearest desires had come to nothing, and when just after Plato's death Aristotle wrote about him, Plato's happiness was most vivid in his memory.

No one who has read Plato feels any surprise that it was so. His singular power, hardly equaled and never surpassed, is that of seeing everything as "a spectator of all time and all existence." The phrase is his own, but he is not speaking of himself; he never does that except in a few letters. He is describing the true philosopher, "a gentle and noble nature" who "desires all truth" and who "seeks to be like God as far as that is possible for man." With not a thought of himself he is drawing his own portrait.

A gentle and noble nature keeping always the perspective of the universal and the eternal, desiring all truth and all goodness, is imprinted on everything he wrote. Never was there a writer so determinedly anonymous. What he thought he put into the mouths of others, but he could not be concealed. The loftiness and beauty that were in him shine out and betray him through all his efforts to hide. He was happy, Aristotle said. Why not? He had reached the source of beauty and truth and goodness. "There is no way of putting it into words," he wrote. "Acquaintance with it must come after a long period of close companionship, when suddenly, like a blaze kindled by a leaping spark, it is born in the soul. ... Then at last, in a flash, understanding blazes up and the mind as it exerts all its powers to the limit of human capacity is flooded with light." Plato had his reward.

Personal griefs and disappointments, the failure of his life's ambition, could not trouble his serenity. His passion of longing to bring about the good state had come to nothing; his cherished plans had failed, but the good had not failed. One of the speakers in the Republic having listened to the description of the wonderful city where the wise and the good should be in sure control, declared, "I do not believe this state of yours has any existence except in words." "Perhaps" was the answer, "a pattern of it is laid up in heaven *for him who wants to see*. But in truth it does not matter if it exists or ever will exist. A man can order his life by its laws."

Aristotle

The Academy was twenty years old when Aristotle entered it. Plato was then about sixty, Aristotle in his late teens. No great philosophical mind had as yet been discovered in the school, but the possibility that he might be was always present. There was an atmosphere of expectation in those quiet halls of learning. The stage was set for the appearance of genius, for the great drama of the supreme philosopher who would take all knowledge for his province and change the course of the world. That he might come and not be recognized did not occur to anyone. It was unthinkable that the Academy instituted to discover and foster genius could fail to discern it when it appeared.

And then one day a seventeen-year-old lad applied for admission and was accepted — and unnoticed. No outward sign marked him, no inward vision of his powers was vouchsafed to anyone. Indeed, it was rather the other way around, for the newcomer was from a small town, little Stagira on the northeast border of Greece, with all the disadvantages that that meant in the eyes of an Athenian. No doubt Aristotle felt shy in that very superior gathering and was glad to be undistinguished. It is highly probable that he was content to have it that way for a long time. He had found someone to whom he could give his utmost devotion and that

seems to have sufficed him for almost all of the twenty
years Plato was still to live. It is an extraordinary length
of time for genius to remain in leading strings. To be
sure, they were very loose strings and restrained him
in one way only, that they were held by one who com-
manded his deepest reverence and affection and admiration. He was completely free to go another way if he
chose, leave his master and follow his own path. There
were no fixed dogmas in the Academy; everything was
open to discussion, to attack and defense. No one claimed
to be teaching the truth; all were seeking it.

Plato dominated Aristotle during those years not
by any conscious exercise of his powers, but by the unconscious influence inevitably exercised by one in whom
the very great and the very good meet. Naturally —
that is, according to the demands of his own nature —
Aristotle's path to the truth was not Plato's. He belonged
to another order.

This basic difference between the two comes out
perpetually in their writings. Through Plato Aristotle
came to believe in God, but Plato never attempted to
prove His reality. Aristotle had to do so. Plato contemplated Him; Aristotle produced arguments to demon-
strate Him. Plato never defined Him, but Aristotle
thought God through logically and concluded with
entire satisfaction to himself that He was the Unmoved
Mover. Plato said, "To find the Father and Creator of

all is hard, and having found Him it is impossible to utter Him." Mystery Aristotle rejected. To him the unknown was to be investigated as quickly and thoroughly as possible and then clearly explained. When the process was applied to God He became the rational center of an orderly universe. To Plato "The wing of the soul" is renewed by dwelling upon the good, the true, the beautiful, and "is raised about the manikins of earth, waiting in wonder to know . . . what God in this life or another may reveal to her."

They agreed little better on terrestrial matters. In regard to the labor question, even more important to the ancient world than to us with our machinery, they saw things differently. A laborer in those days was a slave, and Aristotle thought slavery not only a necessary institution, but one rooted in human nature and therefore beneficent and permanent. "It is clear," he says, "that some men are by nature free and others slaves, and that for the latter slavery is both expedient and right," and he proceeds as always to define: "A slave is a machine which breathes, a piece of animated property." There could not be a statement more comfortable to a slave-owner. Plato could not look at the matter comfortably. In his last book, the Laws, which is concerned with what is immediately practicable as well as what is right, he discusses the way slaves should be treated, but he is not easy in his mind. "A slave is an embarrassing possession," he says. "Many a man has found his slaves better in every way than his brothers or his sons. Slaves have saved their masters' lives and property." Certainly the only way to treat them is to do more justice to them, if that is possible, than to our equals. Further than that he did not go in the Laws, but earlier when he had designed his ideal state he had planned it without slaves. He did not admit them to the Republic. To Aristotle it was impossible to conceive of a civilization without them. The wings of his imagination were not strong enough for a flight into pure ideality away from such a vitally important actuality.

These two ardent seekers of truth who discovered truth for men as no man ever did more, sought and found it by different paths. Plato was the greatest philosopher of the western world; he was also a great artist and he was profoundly religious. Aristotle was the born scientist. He had a burning curiosity about facts, with which Plato was very little concerned. He wanted to know what the world actually was, this natural world which no one had ever looked at before with the eyes of the mind, and he had an unequaled power to bring every bit of knowledge into connection with every other bit, to create order in all that came before him. But this intense curiosity and this extraordinary power remained in abeyance until he was nearing forty and Plato died. For almost twenty years he was a Platonist, believing that knowledge meant knowledge of the good or of God and was independent of all experience. It could be attained only by one who shared in it, that is, as Plato described it, by one "who was as like God as mortal man can be." Plato had attained it. He knew the truth not because he had thought his way through to it, but because he was akin to it and had seen it. "Philosophers," he said, "are lovers of the vision of truth." He had had a vision of God.

Aristotle did not have visions. He could not conceivably have had them. They were inexplicable and they did not explain anything. Aristotle dismissed them on both counts. But he could not dismiss Plato. He lived twenty years with a man who revealed God by being "as like God as mortal man can be," and Aristotle accepted the revelation. As his life went on he became more and more occupied with the things that are seen, but he never forgot that to him whom he had honored beyond all others only the things that are not seen had been important. They grew to be of first importance to him, too. He brought together Plato's world of values which centered in God and his own world of facts.

A great Greek scholar, Professor Jaeger, says that this was Aristotle's unique achievement. He alone united the world of scientific thought and the world of metaphysical thought which is made up of philosophy and art and religion. He brought the two together and held them together as no one else has done. The world of facts, he said in effect, rightly understood, declared the glory of God. "The immeasurable marvel of reality" led him who marveled at it to the Creator of it.

As Plato had had in Socrates a glimpse of the divine shining through a human being, so Aristotle had had in Plato, and it never left him. When he is discussing embryology — or optics — or botany — or anything and everything upon the earth, he will suddenly speak of "the voice of God within us," or of "learning to know God through the divine within us." "Nor ought we to pay regard to those who exhort us that as men we ought to think human things and keep our eyes upon mortality: nay, as far as may be we should endeavor to rise to that which is immortal and live in conformity with that which is best in us." He admonishes his pupils — evidently some of them had objected to dealing with earthworms and the like — "We must not recoil with childish aversion from the examination of the humbler animals. Every realm of nature is marvelous and all will reveal to us something beautiful." This is the voice of Plato's pupil, not the voice of the scientist. Aristotle is not at this point considering particular things in order to classify them. He is thinking of what cannot be analyzed and classified, of what Plato calls "the irradiation of the particular by the general," through a glimpse of the ultimate general, "beauty absolute, simple, and everlasting."

If he had not met Plato it is certainly probable that classification would have been enough and the world would have been his laboratory. It is certain that, when Plato died, he changed. Indeed, the change had begun a few years earlier. From that time on he became more and more the observer and the analyzer, the lover of the factual. He did nothing less than start a revolution in the use of the mind. Before him brilliant men, Plato among them, had pondered over questions of vital human importance such as, for example, the momentous matter of the right constitution for a state. All had considered it in the same way, using the intellect alone, reasoning and thinking out what were the best standards and the best ways of applying them. But when Aristotle wrote a book about the state he had studied the constitutions of a hundred and fifty-eight states. He said in effect: "You cannot find out what is best by thought alone. Observation and experience are necessary as well as logical reasoning and intuitive knowledge." This conception was to affect the basic thinking of the western world. One man before Aristotle had caught a glimpse of it, Hippocrates, the father of modern medicine, but he applied it only to the care of the sick with never an idea that it could apply in other fields as well. First with Aristotle facts became intellectually important. Wherever the intellect could go he went basing explanation on experience, ranging all the way from optics to poetry, from astronomy to ethics, from mathematics to politics, and above all to biology, where his observations were so exhaustive and so accurate that he remained first in the field up to Darwin.

But always he brought his world of fact into connection with Plato's world of truth. To the end of his life Plato never let him go. As has been said, he could shake off Plato's philosophy, but not Plato's God. Something of what Plato was comes to us through the change which living with him brought about in a mind so great and so fundamentally unlike his own.

It is very generally assumed that the influence was all on one side; Aristotle, much younger and comparatively undistinguished, would surely not be able to give to such a one as Plato. But what might well be true in the case of lesser men does not apply to these two. Powers like Aristotle's could not stay hid through years of close living together and powers like Plato's for discerning greatness were to all intents and purposes infallible. When Plato was nearing eighty Aristotle had passed beyond youth, he was in his thirties. It is not credible that he had no influence. There is a marked contrast between Plato's earlier dialogues, the main body of his work, and the later, a small group of five or six. The earlier are the work of a great artist, poetic and full of beauty; the later are dry, closely reasoned writing, perhaps not as dry as the greater part of Aristotle's,

but treatises in which poetry and beauty would be out
of place. The Laws, Plato's last book, stands midway
between the Republic, written years earlier, and Aristotle's book on the state, written after those one hundred and fifty-eight constitutions had been collected.
Plato himself declares that he has moved nearer to the
factual. The Laws, he says, will consider not the ideal
state as did the Republic, but only the second-best, the
more practicable. He is turning away from his almost
lifelong conviction that the only subject worthy of serious consideration is what ought to be. He purposes now
to consider what can be. This change took place when
he was an old man living with a young man at the height
of his extraordinary powers whose chief interest lay in
what is.

A little fragment has come down to us, a mere sentence written by Aristotle shortly before his death, which
gives a final point to the other side of the picture, how
Plato influenced him. Often in the old days when he
was happy in the Academy he had heard Plato illustrate
or describe a spiritual truth, immortality or the soul or
the life of the world to come, by telling a story. He
was nothing of a prophet, he would say to his listeners,
he was making the tale up, but the truth could be seen
in an allegory sometimes better than in a statement, "and
will save us if we are obedient to the word spoken. Thus
shall we live dear to one another and the gods, both here

and when, like conquerors in the games, we receive our reward." The Greek word Plato uses for the story or the word spoken is myth. To us it connotes unreality; it did not to the Greek. Aristotle was thinking of the truth Plato had taught him to see in a myth, in a story, in a poetic expression, and he wrote: "The more lonely and alone I am the more I have come to love myths." Through his life he had loved more and more the factual truth. At the end he loved Plato's truth, which is one with beauty and goodness and could be expressed in some measure, Plato said, only by art, music, poetry, myths.

Chapter V

DEMOSTHENES

THE YEAR Isocrates urged peaceful isolation upon the Athenians saw the first entry into politics of Demosthenes. He was fifty years younger than Isocrates, still a young man in his early thirties, and he had spent his life hitherto in the law courts. What made him leave the law and come forward as a political leader was Athens' imminent danger. Suddenly, it seems, he was awakened to it. The time was just after Athens had been defeated in a war waged to force important allies not to leave her. She was so impoverished by her defeat that there was no money in the treasury, and so feared and hated on all sides that she was friendless and isolated. Isocrates thought her one chance of surviving, of keeping her independence, was to withdraw and take no part in foreign affairs.

The danger at the moment came not from the hostile Greek states, but from two great powers which

were threatening the whole of Greece, not only Athens
— Persia, the hereditary enemy, and a new foe re-
cently grown very strong, the kingdom of Macedon, on
Greece's northern border. It was to the Macedonian king,
Philip, the father of Alexander the Great, that Isocrates
appealed to lead all Greece in a holy war against Persia.
That was not the way Demosthenes saw the matter. His
view of it changed him from a brilliant lawyer matching
wits with other brilliant lawyers into a leader such as
Greece had never known before and was never to know
again. History, indeed, has known few of them.

His point of view was uncomplicated, easily grasped
by the man in the street. There were no uncertainties
to blur the vision. Athens' enemy was not Persia, but
Macedon. Persia was across the sea, Macedon near, ter-
ribly near. Persia was making no threatening moves.
Philip was preparing to conquer not only Athens but
Greece, and the Athenians must be prepared to defend
it and die for it. That was his policy complete. Of course,
he told them, they must get other Greeks to join them
— Philip had a large and admirable fighting force — but
only for this crucial emergency. There was never a
thought in Demosthenes' mind of a future United States
of Greece or even of Greek states coming together in a
confederacy. He was not hoping for anything bigger
and better. The two qualities seldom went together to
a Greek. All Demosthenes wanted was allies to help

Athens put down "the Macedonian wretch." It was a simple, easily understood program which presented almost insuperable practical difficulties such as changing Athens' ages-old enemies into her allies and making over the indifferent and discouraged Athenians into fighters.

Astonishingly he carried it through. The Athenians he had to deal with were easy-going, bent on their own private interests, living very comfortably, employing mercenaries to fight for them and man their ships for them. He turned them into — he talked them into — an army of patriots ready to die for their country. Athens choose safety first? he thundered to them. Never was safety won that way. Only brave citizens made a state safe. Any other way led to certain spiritual degradation, certain failure and defeat. It was better for a nation to be blotted out than live insulted and dishonored. Athens would never slink out of the race and abandon the cause of freedom and lead a kind of existence on sufferance by appeasing or submitting to the powerful.

Demosthenes is a strange figure as he stands in the Assembly in fourth-century Athens pouring forth words of fire. He belongs to another age; he is a hundred years too late. There were very great men in Athens at that time, men of lofty nobility, his equals in character, even his superiors, men of intellect beyond his power to fathom, and men of patriotism which even his pure and deep passion for his country could not surpass, but of them all he alone was heroic. He was a hero and there were no more in Athens. Heroism is active and the outstanding Athenians when the city's time of trouble came were men of thought, not action. There was Plato, a genius never yet surpassed. He would no longer turn that genius upon the affairs of the state. He would not go on trying to help what his mind told him was beyond the reach of help. He withdrew. The same was true to a still greater degree of Aristotle. He never even entered political life as Plato once had done. He was content, or at the very least resigned, to use his mighty intellect in the laboratory while Athens came nearer and nearer to the loss of what had been life's chief value to her, freedom, independence. And there was Isocrates, at long last convinced that war was unalleviated evil and peace the only condition upon which Athens could survive.

That was how Athenians of highest character and greatest intellect saw the situation. Demosthenes got no help from any of them. What he did all alone was almost miraculous. He fired that soft, irresponsible, apathetic mass of city folk to take up arms and fight to the death. He won over Greek states that had been bitter enemies of Athens to join her. He literally called into being by his tremendous eloquence a national uprising against Macedon, something that had never happened in Greece except in the days of Marathon and Salamis. As he talked old barriers of hatred that kept the country divided fell away. It was Isocrates' dream of Greek union realized, but against Philip, not for him. Perhaps most wonderful of all, he lifted the whole political mess which Plato had turned from as hopeless, out of the corruption in which it was sunk up to a lofty level of patriotism. What Isocrates had all his life tried in vain to do, Demosthenes did.

That is why he has lived through the years and his name is known wherever Greece is known, along with Homer's and Pericles' and Plato's. He is not immortal because of wonderfully fashioned orations, because of admirable excellence as a stylist, although scholar after scholar has insisted ever since scholarship began that there lies his true claim, in his beautiful rhythmic language and balanced phrases and unerring choice of words. More than that is needed for immortality. He stands in the front rank of Greece not because of an eloquent tongue and an elegant style. He is there with the men who fell at Thermopylae and all the others who have so acted as to raise the standard for the world of what brave men can do.

He was unsuccessful by the ordinary standards of judgment. Under his guidance — not his command, he fought as a common soldier — the Athenians and their allies took the road of hardship and self-sacrifice, met Philip's army at Chaeronea and were overwhelmingly defeated. Demosthenes escaped from the battlefield with the other fugitives when all was over. He must have longed to stay and die, but made as he was he could not drop the burden of his leadership. His place was in Athens full of mourning for those whom he had led to death. He went back, but to find that in one sense he had not failed. Under him the Athenians had ascended to a point where far from reproaching and blaming him they defended him, refusing again and again to give him up to Philip or Alexander or any Macedonian. That is a glorious period in the history of Athens just before she steps out of history.

Demosthenes was practically alone in what he did. One man raised up a city, a country, to fight for liberty or death. The fact that he could do it illustrates the strange power of faith which history must reckon with. Demosthenes was possessed by an absolute faith in the power of the good. He believed that force based on wrongdoing could be at most only superficially strong. It had a fatal core of weakness which must in the end bring it down. Men fighting for freedom could fight in full confidence because the right could never suffer a real defeat. Philip's power was evil. He was a despot seeking to extend his despotism over free peoples. It was impossible that he should succeed and the slavish subjects of a tyrant should conquer free men fighting for their country.

This faith which burned in him was what he fired

the Greeks with. It may seem based upon sheer unreality, but that is not true, it has a solid foundation. It is a historical fact that faith has moved mountains. Heroism is never rational and every heroic life and death is a challenge to cool reason's pronouncing that it is folly to attempt the impossible. Heroes have attempted it and have succeeded; essentially indeed, they are never defeated, not by Philip of Macedon or anyone else. Every heroic death, as Sir Walter Scott said, sends down an imperious challenge to the generations to come.

Years after Chaeronea, years of subjection to Macedon, in his last and perhaps his greatest speech Demosthenes expressed the faith of his life as he never had when Athens was free and hope was bright. To the Athenians, helpless subjects of a hated power, he reviewed his leadership and he defended it: "I declare that if we had foreseen what would happen the city ought to have taken the course she did if she had any regard for honor, for her tradition, for the judgment of posterity. It is true that she is judged as having failed. Well, that is the common lot of all when heaven wills. But if we had betrayed Greece to Philip without a struggle, we who have never preferred inglorious safety to peril with honor — how could we have looked a stranger in the face? We could have kept our own in peace if we had been willing to obey orders and suffer another to be head of Greece. But that was not possible. It is not in our nature to side with an evil man because he is powerful and embrace subjection because it is safe. You failed, men of Athens, but you were not in the wrong when you did battle for freedom. I swear it by those who fought at Marathon, at Salamis, and many more who died for our country and whom she honors even when conquered.

"And rightly, for though their fate was decreed by a higher power, all of them, victor and vanquished alike, did what brave men can do."

The words, Grote says, are Athens' funeral oration. After Alexander's death Athens rose up a second time against the Macedonians and suffered her final defeat. Again Demosthenes was foremost in urging her to fight. After the battle he killed himself so as not to fall into the hands of the enemy. He could do no more for Athens, which at the very end was forced to agree to give him up to the Macedonians. Sophocles' Ajax says as he falls on his sword because he will not live dishonored, "A man can live nobly or die nobly." So all Greeks thought. When Demosthenes died he believed that he was joining the great company who, "victors and vanquished alike, did what brave men can do."

Chapter VI

ALEXANDER THE GREAT

THERE IS something breath-taking in Alexander The Great's Empire. Like everything stupendous — the pyramids, the Grand Canyon, Mt. Everest — one can never get quite used to it. It drives us out beyond the everyday limits we set for ourselves of the possible. There is a fairy-tale quality, too, in the swiftness of its creation. In eleven years Alexander made himself master of the immense stretch of land from the Adriatic into India and across the Indus, from upper Egypt to the northernmost point of the Black Sea, from the Indian Ocean to the Caspian; almost as big as the Roman Empire at its height after a thousand years of fighting.

This extraordinary conqueror had an extraordinary education. His father got for him the most remarkable tutor that ever tutored anyone. Aristotle taught him for a number of years. His father, Philip, king of Macedon, induced the great man to leave Greece and put

Alexander in his hands when he was about thirteen. Plutarch tells us that he did not let them live with him but sent them off to a little town where they were practically alone together, an unschooled boy in his early teens and one of the greatest minds the world has ever known. Alexander's wonderful good fortune in this turn of events has been dwelt upon by practically everyone who has written about him, but clearly there is another side to the matter.

The master of those who know had only one person to talk to. This was undoubtedly hard on him, but it was also hard on the thirteen-year-old boy. Aristotle was a scientist and a philosopher and a logician and a critic and an economist and a historian and an authority on ethics, and a master in every field he entered. Education too had engaged his attention. It was he who defined liberal subjects of study as opposed to utilitarian, and he had theories about the proper combination of the two. There is however no indication in what we know of him that when he was presented with Alexander he had ever had to put theory into practice, not even with the young considered as a class, much less with one definite young creature. Even that mighty mind must have felt unsure just at first until the habit of his life reasserted itself and he could go back comfortably to his own intellectual world. Inevitably one sees him pacing the road before the house — in Athens his custom was to walk while he lectured — talking about what was uppermost in his thoughts at the moment, with Alexander occasionally listening and wondering what it was all about, then diverted by some country sight or sound, then slipping away without the lecturer noticing that a small boy was missing.

Of all the subjects he listened to Alexander liked literature best. The historians gravely assure us that Aristotle's success as a teacher is proved by his pupil becoming a lover of Homer, but in those circumstances the Iliad must have seemed an oasis in the desert. That the subject he liked next best was biology is only a conjecture, but it is reasonable. Aristotle was the greatest biologist up to modern times and when he described the life of the bee or the development of the chick in the egg, the boy could follow him easily as he could not when the syllogism was the subject or inductive reasoning or the Prime Mover Unmoved. His subsequent history seems to prove that he was really interested when his teacher talked about human beings as the scientist sees them, not divided into Greeks and barbarians, but as a division of the great class of living creatures, occupying the highest place in that class, all of them, of whatever nationality. That idea Alexander's mind seized upon and kept. The historians also say that Aristotle told him that Asiatics were slaves by nature. At that moment he had laid the biologist aside and the historian was considering Asiatic political history which pointed that way as it had always done. One wonders if he ever took the trouble to find out the shape his discourses were taking in that young mind, so keen, so impressionable and so obstinate. As they lived together amicably and parted with great friendliness it seems probable that he did not and that Alexander drew his own conclusions unopposed. By the time Aristotle left him they were convictions never to be changed.

The state his mind had reached after these years of talk he had full opportunity to show when his father died and he became king. There was no one now to oppose any ideas that had struck him. They were not many. Foremost was the notion that everybody was like everybody else. He must have got this from Aristotle's biology. He could have got it nowhere else. The Greek mind of the day had not yet considered the unity of the human race, and it is not credible that Alexander himself conceived it. He was not a thinker; he was a passionate lover of action, preferably violent action, happiest in battle, glorying in danger, an adventurer in every sense of the word. Really to think, to follow out seriously a train of thought, would have bored him past endurance if it had ever occurred to him to try.

What he did do was to listen to Aristotle talk about the classification of living creatures and get firmly fixed in his mind that there were no real differences in the

class of human beings. He took this over unmodified by
any such considerations as the actual and visible differences between nations. Aristotle had distinguished between the nature of peoples who sought for freedom and
those who acquiesced in slavery, but Alexander had
not listened. He had a burning ambition to surpass, to
be the first, in Macedon, in Greece, in Asia, over the
whole earth, and he saw with a glowing spirit One
World, to be brought into union by himself. It was well
for Aristotle's peace of mind that he could not read
what was in that young head when the two took leave
of each other. It is easy to picture the weight of calm
logic with which he would have annihilated Alexander's
one world.

But left to himself Alexander happily dismissed
racial and national distinctions. They were unimportant.
They could be wiped out easily by a man who set about
it in the right way. All he had to do was to conquer a
nation thoroughly and then make it follow the desired
pattern. The matter presented itself to him as simply as
that. His immediate goal was to bring together those
hereditary foes, Greece and Persia, not merely with
Isocrates' idea that Persia was to receive Greek civilization, but also that Greece was to be orientalized, a first
step toward uniting East and West. Before that, of
course, Persia must be conquered. Isocrates' plan of a
sacred military mission to Persia bringing only good in

its train was not Alexander's idea of the way to conquer, but he intended when he had carried out his conquest, killed numberless thousands, seized the wealth, reduced all to helplessness, then to shower Greek blessings on the people and make them love Greeks. Something like this was in his mind when he set out for Asia.

The plan of invading the East was not his. He inherited it from his father, Philip. Philip was a first-rate general and had built up a first-rate fighting force. When he decided to become the champion of the West in the ages-old contest he certainly knew Xenophon's account of how a little Greek army had shown up the real weakness of oriental magnificence. Xenophon's Ten Thousand had marched to the interior of Persia and had marched out again and got back home in spite of all the efforts made to destroy them. Philip was a man of great intelligence. He concluded that the conquest of the East was entirely practicable, and in addition to the glory the conqueror would win, to him a matter of far less importance than it became to his son, there was the prospect of illimitable plunder. The riches of the Orient were fabulous. Isocrates' idea of bringing to the barbarian the blessings of Greek culture did not in all probability play a large part in his mind.

Before he started he wasted no time trying to persuade the Greeks to act with him. He had been dealing with them, sometimes as an enemy, sometimes as a friend, for twenty-five years, and he knew that it would be fatal to depend upon a union of Greeks for any cause whatever. He took the only practical way to make his rear safe by conquering Greece first. That was all he could do, however. He was assassinated on the eve of his departure and his project fell to his son.

Alexander was little more than a boy, only twenty or so, when he set off to conquer the world. It was a boy's dream made into a brief semblance of reality by an amazing young man who not only had supreme confidence in himself, but was able to inspire multitudes of men with the same confidence. He could make people believe in him to a degree hardly surpassed in history. Plutarch who admired him beyond all others so that any criticism he makes of him is at once accepted by the reader, paints him as uncontrolled and undependable, with an unquenchable thirst for excitement, conceited beyond measure and rash beyond calculation, nevertheless a leader of men, endowed with the great leader's strange power to get others to do whatever he wishes.

Not many of the world's great leaders have used Alexander's methods. He made his army follow him on perilous adventures and terrifying marches into the unknown by making them feel that he was one with them, sharing their hardships and dangers, literally leading them, always foremost in the battle. Obstacles, perils, hardships, only stimulated him and in terrible situations he could infect his men with his own soaring spirit because they knew he would always do more than he asked of them. There are many tales about his complete and careless courage. Danger had as irresistible an attraction for him as for any hero of romance.

In those early days, he showed himself again and again to be the perfect knight-errant. During a journey through a burning desert when the water supply failed and the army was almost dying of thirst a man offered him a skin full of water. Alexander took it; then looking at the thirsty soldiers around him he gave it back saying, "There is not enough for all." Of course his men adored him.

No one, not Arthur or Galahad, could have improved upon his behavior to the wife of Darius whom he captured. He restored all her treasures of gold and jewels and sent her word that he would not come into her presence unless she summoned him. A king whom he took captive when he was advancing into India showed a haughty defiance in his presence and Alexander, interested, asked him, "How shall I treat you?" "As a king," answered the other with the result that Alexander restored to him the kingdom he had just taken from him. Once when he was ill and his physician was mixing a draught for him, a letter was brought to him from his most trusted general telling him that the physician had been bribed by the Persian king to poison him.

Alexander raised the draught to his lips with one hand and with the other gave the letter to the physician. By the time the letter had been read the medicine had been drunk. No harm was done; the physician was trustworthy, but Alexander appears here in his true colors. He was the adventurer complete. He loved to stake his all upon a chance. He was a gay gambler with life, almost to the end.

It is quite possible that none of these stories are true, but they were told about him by men who knew him, to be read by other men who knew him. At the very least they are characteristic, the sort of thing people learned to expect of him. One of his biographers, Arrian, puts the case clearly after describing something specially heroic, "If it so happened, I have nothing but praise for Alexander. If the historians told it because they thought it the sort of thing Alexander would do, I still have only praise for Alexander." The picture drawn of his early days is that of a young man with an overflowing, impulsive generosity, very attractive and in strong contrast with what he became only a few years later.

Our sources for Alexander's life are four writers who lived between four and five hundred years after him. Nothing has come down to us of the sources they used, but we know that three of them were lives written by officers in Alexander's army. Of the four authorities we have, two are unimportant, but fortunately for us one of the other two is Plutarch, a great writer and a man of sound judgment. Arrian, who belongs with him, has also notable good sense and, as the quotation given above shows, does not accept his authorities unquestioningly.

All the way to Babylon the army had only victories and none of them costly. Egypt yielded without a blow, so did far distant Cyrene, neighbor to Carthage. One city after another in Asia Minor surrendered on demand with but two exceptions quickly reduced to helplessness. Tyre alone offered a real resistance and delayed Alexander several months. But that was the only check. The Persian armies were defeated, the king killed, his treasure strongholds seized, with astonishing ease. Mighty Babylon of the tremendous walls threw open her gates on his arrival. Magnificent Susa did the same. If here was a man bent on conquering the world, here also was a world ready to be conquered.

When the army left Babylon for the Far East, matters changed. Hardships increased, plunder lessened, above all they were advancing into the absolutely unknown. Nevertheless, they kept on. They went over the Hindu Kush mountains into Bactria, an extraordinarily difficult exploit, and later crossed them again on the way to India. The farther east they went the fiercer grew the fighting, but no defeats have come down to us.

They entered India and passed over the river Indus. According to Alexander's notions of geography they were by now very near to the end of the world, which of course he desired ardently to reach. And then, with the goal almost within his grasp as he thought, the soldiers refused to go on. The army told their general they wanted no more conquests and were going home. It cannot be doubted that he brought everything he had, all his authority, all his great personal power, to bend them to his will. He did not change them.

This remarkable mutiny is treated as unimportant by our authorities, Plutarch and Arrian, but both make it clear that the early biographers they depended on were bent upon glorifying their subject. Plutarch says he drew from them the conclusion that Alexander was of heroic strength and beauty and that "his body was so fragrant as to perfume the clothes he wore." Writers like that would pass quickly over a black blot on their hero's fair fame such as a successful revolt of his troops. The mutiny is very important. It marks the beginning of a break between him and the Greeks.

We do not hear of any violence connected with the rebellion. The difference was peacefully settled. The army had its way, but Alexander continued to be their leader. It was a curious situation, but as Xenophon shows in the Anabasis, a Greek soldier was a Greek first and a soldier only second, and Alexander's troops were quite aware of the predicament they were in and that their best way out lay in the military genius of their commander. They would not obey him in regard to the advance, but they knew that they could trust him as no one else to devise the best means for the retreat, and they returned to all appearances the same disciplined army which had started out. There is not a hint of any trouble, much less another mutiny, through the great dangers and sufferings of the journey back. There is not a hint either that anyone thought this behavior remarkable. It was to be expected that a Greek army in difficulties would use their heads and act reasonably.

Nevertheless, it is not to be supposed that Alexander forgave and forgot. He who had never been opposed before had been forced to yield to his own soldiers and give up his dearest desire. He kept his resentment to himself on the march back, but after he reached Babylon the relation between himself and the army changed.

There had been difficulties even before they left Babylon. It had become evident that the great plan of uniting the West and the East was up against a real obstacle. Alexander was finding it very difficult to orientalize his Macedonians. He himself adopted easily and quickly oriental ways. He dressed in gorgeous Persian robes — after all, he was very young and very handsome — and he lived after the fashion of a Persian despot, which was an exceedingly pleasant way of life. But the

Greek soldiers did not like it. Greek ways were good enough for them. In point of fact they felt themselves immensely superior to the conquered, as all conquerors have always done except Alexander only. His present aim was to become a Persian to the Persians, and for the moment he gave little thought to the much less agreeable task of remaining a Greek to the Greeks.

Of course it was difficult to steer a course between the Orientals and the Westerners. Undoubtedly the Persians would have despised a king who lived in simple Greek fashion. But however that may be, no explanation is needed for the pleasure the young conqueror took in the splendor and luxury that surrounded him. Plutarch says that on one of his journeys he and his friends reveled day and night upon a lofty platform drawn by horses and covered with embroidered purple canopies. All were crowned with garlands, all drank the costliest of wines, while music resounded and women danced. It seems the dream paradise of a boy who has just read the Arabian Nights, but it is probably a vivid picture of the extravagances of an oriental court, perpetually trying to banish boredom by more and more of the same thing. After a course in this kind of entertainment the ways of Greece must have looked very unattractive to him.

Then Alexander had himself proclaimed a god-king, which would not especially shock Greeks brought up on Homer's Olympians, and yet it was foreign to their way of thinking. They never had much use for strictly human kings, and notions of their divinity or of the divine right of kings, never entered their minds. Apparently when the proclamation of his godhood reached Greece it was not received quite as Alexander would have had it. The Spartans said, "If Alexander likes to call himself a god we have no objection." But the Greeks in Persia greatly objected to his order that all who approached him should prostrate themselves. Aristotle's grandnephew drew down on himself Alexander's lasting enmity by asking him: "On your return to Greece will you compel Greeks, the only free men among all mankind, to fall down before you? Will you inflict this shame on Macedonians?" But Alexander would not give way. He treated with extreme severity anyone who refused, even leaping up from his throne and with his own hands dashing against the wall a Macedonian who had burst into roars of laughter at the spectacle.

All in all, before the mutiny the army and their commander were drifting apart on the all-important question of West versus East. During the long march from Greece to Babylon Alexander had shown himself properly desirous of bringing Greek ways to Persia. As he advanced he planned Greek towns along the line of march, each complete with Greek columns and Greek names (usually Alexandria). In all of them Greeks were to be the authority and Greek the official language, but Greek freedom was not contemplated as part of their equipment. Alexander was to be absolute lord of them all. He is said to have created — out of nothing — seventy such cities, but every reader by the time he reaches this point has become cautious about accepting marvels. Still, it is beyond question that a number of such towns did spring up as he marched on, all in his mind to be dispensers of Greek culture to that vast hostile land. Plutarch gives Alexander's idea of how they were to do it: "As soon as Alexander subdued Asia, Homer became an author in high repute and young men in Persia sang the tragedies of Sophocles and Euripides."

Thus when he reached Babylon half of the plan he had in mind when he left Greece was at any rate well begun, and on this point the army were in full sympathy with his views. After he returned from India he proceeded to put into effect another and more drastic plan, intermarriage between the two nations. This was an unheard-of procedure. Greeks did not marry foreigners under penalty of losing their citizenship, an inestimable loss. Anyone who so offended became a man without a country and his children the same, a terrible fate in the ancient world. The superiority of Greeks to all other nations was proudly and effectively maintained. Alexander rejected it. It is impossible to say when the idea came to him that intermarriage would be a final

solvent of the racial distinctions which it was his lofty
mission to end, but it seems probable that the keen pleasure he took in the Persian way of life and in the companionship of Persians made it increasingly convincing
to him. When he came back from the East he thought
the moment ripe for it; to troops who had carried out a
successful mutiny it would be a diversion and a piece
of good policy. He went to Susa, one of the most
splendid of Persian cities, and there he gave a grand
marriage feast. The soldiers were encouraged and bribed
to marry Persian women. Alexander led the way. According to Plutarch he married the daughter of the
dead Persian king; according to Arrian two Persian
ladies of royal blood. His friends and officers followed
his example. The festival was magnificent. Nine thousand guests were present, to each of whom he gave a
golden cup.

But Alexander had not forgotten or forgiven. Before he started for the Far East he had arranged to have
thirty thousand young Persians made over into a proper
disciplined force. Now he put them into the army on an
equality with the Greeks, an inevitable source of perpetual dissension and weakened discipline, which Alexander certainly was aware of and as certainly had pro-
vided for. His next step was to send the Greek soldiers
home, beginning with the disabled. It would seem that
he had decided he could depend upon the Persians

and could not upon the Greeks. According to Plutarch there was a terrible uproar. The Greeks were not taken in by his order that only the sick and maimed should go. They knew he was planning to get rid of them all, and they besieged his tent begging him to keep them. Plutarch glides over just how the matter was finally settled. He says only that Alexander "dismissed those that were unserviceable with munificent rewards."

By the time they left, the end of this blazing comet-like life was near. He had planned, Plutarch says, to make the world Greek. What happened was that he turned Persian. Nothing is clearer than that he had lost whatever of Greek excellence he had had in him by nature or by education. Moderation, reasonableness, self-control, had gone. One story after another has come down of friends he ordered killed and killed himself, of sudden drunken furies when he took terrible reprisals, of horrible ways he used of inflicting death, all in strict accordance with the procedures of oriental royalty. Aristotle's grandnephew, who had remonstrated with him on that matter of prostrating, he had put to death. The young man was a devoted admirer even though he sometimes criticized him. His foster-brother, who had saved his life more than once, he killed for nothing worse than a taunt when he was drunk. The general most responsible for his victories, the best and most trustworthy of his officers, he caused to be assassinated because his only living son — two others had died in battle fighting for Alexander — was suspected of treachery. He had Bessus, the man who killed the Persian king — hardly the act of an enemy — horribly mutilated and then torn to pieces, acts which are happily absent from Greek history. It was not only in the way he dressed and in the way he lived that he had adopted the East.

A number of modern historians think that to the day of his death he was actively carrying out the grandiose plan of bringing all the races of mankind into one universal brotherhood to which each would contribute the best in its own culture. Thus when he had taught Greeks to love Persian ways, and Persians Greek ways, or at the least when the foundation for this admirable development had been firmly laid, he would proceed to repeat the performance in the other countries. After the East had been well started on the right path he would turn to the West, and the final result would be a wonderful culture embracing all the world. So a number of historians tell us. With this idea of him he changes from the person Plutarch and the other three biographers paint — our only source of knowledge — to a profound thinker possessed by a lofty conception millenniums in advance of his age, and by a truly great man's ambition to confer lasting benefit on mankind. The ancient and the modern historians agree in no respect.

The last glimpse of him the ancient historians give

us shows no trace of the Greek, only the Eastern despot complete. Shortly before his death his most intimate friend died from disobeying his physician's orders. Alexander's grief literally knew no bounds. He crucified the physician; he fell upon a mountain tribe and put them all to the sword as an offering to the dead man's spirit; he set aside millions of money for his tomb. Plutarch says, "He was so beyond all reason transported that to express his sorrow he immediately ordered the manes and tails of all his horses and mules to be cut off and thrown down the battlements of the cities near by." The account fits in well enough with Asia, but Greece has receded to an immeasurable distance.

A few months later he too was dying after two drinking bouts, one of which Plutarch says lasted all night and all the next day. Both Arrian and Plutarch speak of his increasing drunkenness. Arrian says, "Alexander took to barbaric ways of drinking." The fact was widely known. In Athens Menander, the most popular playwright of the day, had one of his characters say to another, "You're drunk — drunker than the king, than Alexander." The other answers, "Not much less, anyway." And the first retorts, "Pretty deep drinking, I'll say." Young though he was, his health could not hold out against wild orgies continually repeated. A violent fever set in and proved fatal. He was thirty-two years old. Arrian's final comment is: "As for what was in

Alexander's mind I do not care to guess, but this I will say that he had no small or mean conceptions, nor would he ever have rested content with what he had won if he had added Europe to Asia and the Britannic Islands to Europe. He was always the rival of his own self."

With all his extraordinary personal power and his equally extraordinary confidence that he could do and dare beyond everyone else, with all his fiery ambitions, his splendid prowess, his disdain of pain and death, he never grew up. When he died he was still a boy, not a Greek boy, however, but sunk in effortless luxury and corrupted into irresponsible cruelty. Conquered Persia had taken captive her conqueror.

Arrian sums it up: "I regard Bessus' mutilation as barbaric. I agree that Alexander was carried away so far as to copy oriental luxury. I hold that no mighty deeds, not even conquering the whole world, is of any good unless the man has learned the mastery of himself."

His death showed the thinness of the Greek veneer he had applied to the unchanging East. The Greek columns in his towns remained; a few are still standing today. The inhabitants became Asiatic. When he died there was chaos. His empire fell to pieces almost before he was buried. His family perished in a riot of murder after the fashion of Orientals upon a change of ruler. All were killed, his little son, his wives, his mother, his brother. His conquests became the prey of his generals.

After bitter warfare, all futile except for the number of people killed, they came to a kind of uneasy agreement and divided the countries between them, but the inevitable quarrels that resulted kept the civilized world in a turmoil for the better part of a century. When a more tranquil age succeeded, the East had reasserted her sway over the lands which Alexander had conquered and plundered in his dream of creating One World.

Chapter VII

MENANDER

WHILE Alexander was fighting and enjoying himself
in the East a boy was growing up in Athens who was to
become one of the two most famous writers of comedy
in the ancient world. His name was Menander and of
all the playwrights he was the best-loved. He was especially popular in Rome. Cicero, an excellent critic, called
the admired Terence "Menander with half lopped off."
Ovid addressed him as "delightful." The greatest critic
of them all, Quintilian, held him up as a model for young
men to study, "so completely has he mirrored human
life." Both the Roman dramatists, Plautus and Terence,
claimed proudly that their dramas were founded on his,
even sometimes to the degree of being copies. An anonymous poet in the Greek Anthology called him "The
bright morning star of the New Comedy"; an Alexan-
drian admirer summed up to perfection the general
opinion of him: "O Life, O Menander, which of you

two was the plagiarist?" Plutarch even declared that he preferred him to Aristophanes, but then it is difficult to think of the decorous Plutarch ever reading Aristophanes.

Not one of his plays has come down to us entire, but we have many scenes, sometimes connected so that the plot can be made out. There are many shorter fragments too, and a great many quotations of a line or so. All in all we have quite enough to know what he was like and also what the audience that applauded him was like.

Antiquity prized him above all for his truth to life, that is, to human nature, but we can get more from him than that. We can see in his mirror Athenian life at the end of the fourth century. His comedy is a true comedy of manners and as such it must deal only with the familiar. Easy entertainment is the aim of such plays and that is at an end if anyone or anything strange is presented and the audience has to puzzle and then, inevitably, feels disapproving. To enjoy themselves they must see characters they understand and life lived as they live it. The people who delighted in Menander saw themselves reflected in his stage. "The drama's laws the drama's patrons give," and the laws the Athenians laid down for his plays show what they themselves were.

Menander was twenty-one years old when Alexander died, and had already brought out one play. As conquerors Philip and Alexander had treated the Athenians leniently, even considerately. Political freedom was at an end, but freedom of speech remained; Menander could make fun of Alexander without fear of unpleasant consequences. He knew the Athenians would enjoy a scoffing reference to the stories of drunken orgies that had found their way across the sea, and that he could find capital matter for a joke, too, in the general opinion that the distinguishing mark of the Great and Glorious, the Superman, was a superhuman conceit:

> How Alexander-like is all this sort of thing,
> "If I want some one he'll appear unsummoned.
> "If I need a pathway over the sea waters
> "The sea will give me footing."

There was no question of censorship for Menander. He could write what he pleased. The only question he had to decide was what would please the Athenians and as Menander saw it, public affairs were not on that list.

The pleasant, well-bred people who made up his audience were bored by politics, and why not? They were the wards of a distant tyranny which interfered, indeed, very little; but they knew, as no men better, the difference between freedom and obedience and they were not going through the motions of self-government when the substance had gone. Even before the Macedonians had conquered them politics were falling into disrepute.

Noisy demagogues made the Assembly a disagreeable place to fastidious people; gross corruption was on the increase; gentlemen were generally disgusted. With Alexander's advent they left the political scene, probably with few regrets.

There is another witness besides Menander to the change that had come over the Athenian people. He is Theophrastus, to whom Aristotle left his school, the Lyceum, when he finally retired in the year of Alexander's death. Menander was one of his pupils. He was, of course, a philosopher and he also wrote many learned works on botany which, as is the way with most learned works, have with the years lost their importance, but he was a keen observer of men as well and he has left us a book which is a series of sketches of people shrewdly and sharply drawn. They are all extremely unpleasant people, not criminal — there is not an out-and-out villain among them — but they make up a vivid picture gallery of the disagreeable and the stupid and the silly individuals that were to be met with on a stroll along the streets of Athens.

Aristophanes' favorite targets of abusive fun, the politically inept and corrupt, are completely absent from the collection. There is only one passage in the book that bears on politics in which an old-fashioned Tory is forever saying, "We should rid ourselves of the mob," "We should give up trying for office," "I marvel that men touch public affairs." He is ashamed when some ill-kempt fellow sits next him in the Assembly, while he himself wears his cloak with studied elegance and has his hair cut to exactly the right length and his fingernails carefully attended to. That is the extent of Theophrastus' dabbling with politics. In his description of the Garrulous Man's endless flow of talk about everything in the world from what he had for supper to the performance of the Mysteries there is not an allusion to political matters. Theophrastus' Athenians were as little concerned with public life as Menander's.

Nevertheless, when the news of Alexander's death and the chaos that followed reached Athens, the city took fire; the citizens rose up and in company with other Greek states defied Macedon. The revolt was quickly put down, but with a burdensome and humiliating result, a Macedonian garrison lodged with them to keep them in order. Then the Athenians definitely retired to private life. "Stay at home," one of Menander's characters says. "A man is free and happy nowhere else." There they were not interfered with. Secret police and concentration camps were unknown and the unpleasantness of the political situation could be forgotten in the comforts of domesticity.

This is the scene Menander paints. His characters are absorbed in domestic affairs to such a degree that there is not a word about anything outside, no matter how important. The year his first play was produced saw the defeat of the uprising to throw off the control of Macedon and the Macedonian garrison installed. It was the year, too, when Demosthenes ended his long struggle against Philip and Alexander and took poison. Zeno, founder of the Stoics, was in Athens by then and so was Epicurus, a close friend of Menander's. Much was going on in the city which by any usual standards would be of interest to everyone, but Menander chose to ignore it all. Except for the two allusions to Alexander there is not a word in what we have of him about one important person or one important event. And yet the Athenians had been used to getting in their theatre a commentary on public life — there were no newspapers — and even to seeing public characters represented on the stage. What Menander's immediate predecessors on the stage did we do not know, nothing they wrote has come down; but Aristophanes' plays were full of grand people, generals, politicians, poets, playwrights, Socrates. To Menander's audience the day for that sort of thing had passed. It was not possible to laugh at politics. Whatever verged on the public scene might be in some way connected with Macedonians and no playwright should remind them of the foreign garrison within their country.

In private life, however, there were plenty of interests, diverting and exciting, first-rate dramatic material. Menander followed his audience there. The background of his stage as far as we can see it, is always the same, a prosperous, well-ordered home, except of course for the temporary disturbances demanded by the drama. When once the complicated network of misunderstandings which makes up the plot is cleared away, the life represented is very pleasant. Ease and luxury are taken for granted. A slave says to his young master,

Insomnia? I dare say — and here's the reason,
How do you live? A stroll around the market
And back you come all tired. Then a nice warm bath.
Food when you feel like eating. Sleep? Your life's a sleep.
So many good things crowd on you, you've got no room
For any ordinary need.

That is the atmosphere of the plays. In all of them the pleasures that money can buy are well to the fore. Of course there are slaves to do everything for everybody and also, a specially luxurious touch, Persian servants whose task is to fan the flies away. No doubt a touch of high fashion, too.

Food is by no means taken for granted. It is a very agreeable addition to life's enjoyments, and we know why. Menus are occasionally given and they sound excellent. We hear of "jellied soups" and "Lydian entrées," and "cakes sweet with honey." A sauce highly commended is made of eggs and honey and a bit of flour. Then there are cheese omelettes and roasted thrush, and "all kinds of fresh fish served with exquisite sauces." A remarkable savory is guaranteed to whet the appetite. Clothes are important, too, and very elegant. Ladies wear "silken robes as delicate as the mist" and dresses "of royal purple brought from Persia" and golden ornaments, too, set with jewels; emeralds are mentioned and pearls. There are silver drinking cups and goblets studded with gems and gold-plated cases in which sandals are kept. Personal habits are extremely fastidious. A father contemplating his son remarks,

> Yes, I *was* young once, but I did not bathe
> Five times a day and use perfumed oil.

Everything outside is ignored. Only a few years before, Isocrates had denounced with passion the unjust way rich people were treated, the people who made up, certainly in large part, Menander's audience, but nobody in the plays ever comments on anything like that. No one even mentions taxes, the subject of some of Isocrates' most fiery words. There must have been a carefully followed convention as to what was and was not admissible in polite conversation. We have too little of Menander to make a list of subjects well-bred people banned, but we can conclude with tolerable certainty that patriotism was one of them. There is not an allusion in any play to Athens, not one word about her past glory, not one expression of devotion to the city that had been so loved in other days. The word freedom is never found. All this is significant because it shows a reversal of a long habit. Up to Menander the Athenians were forever talking about their glorious city of freedom, but his audience had discovered a way to live contentedly under the orders of another country, and the way was to become indifferent to their own.

And yet the people who crowded the theatre were by no means dull or even commonplace. The plays presuppose quick-witted hearers who did not need their i's dotted for them. Subtleties did not have to be underlined or explained. Menander could be sure of a ready understanding when he said, "A fortunate man must nobly bear his blessings," or "He alone learned compassion through prosperity." He knew a delicate bit of character analysis would be appreciated: "Who leads an austere life has a cold heart toward others," and "Who loves most feels most a mere trifling wrong."

There is, indeed, an astonishing amount of high thinking and wise thinking in the lines antiquity quoted and preserved. The people they were addressed to could be counted upon to be instantly caught by anything fine and good. Christ said, "Out of the heart proceed evil thoughts. These are what defile a man." Four hundred years earlier Menander said, "All that defiles a man comes from within." Christ's saying about the beam in one's own eye and the mote in one's neighbor's, Menander anticipated: "When you would say some evil of your neighbor, first think of all the evil in yourself." Hamlet's, "Conscience doth make cowards of us all" is an echo of Menander, "The man who has a load upon his mind — conscience makes him a coward." When St. Paul said, "Evil communications corrupt good manners," he was, whether he knew it or not, directly quoting Menander. His widely acclaimed "This is life, not to live for self" was repeated by writer after writer, as also, "You are a man. Then pray not to be free from sorrow, but for courage that endures." Equal wisdom is in "No man while sinning sees his sin for what it is. Later he sees."

He knew he would not displease his audience when he wrote,

If a man can change a god to that which he desires,
Then he himself is greater than the god.

He did not have to appear conservative in any line. Probably many of his hearers were proud of being independent thinkers, superior to narrow class conceptions, and Menander was free to write his famous

No man is alien to me. In us all
There is one nature.

He could count on an approving laugh when one of his youthful heroes said,

Mother — you're killing me with all these pedigrees,
Reeling off lists of all our grandfathers.
You won't say, will you, there's a man alive
Who hasn't got a grandfather? I tell you,
A man who's good by nature, Mother mine,
Even if he's born an Ethiopian,
Is nobly born.

The attitude in the plays toward slavery is proof enough by itself that the Athenians of the day were not at their ease about slaves. Fifth-century Athens had never given them a thought except for Euripides, the arch-heretic. Plato had felt uncomfortable. To Aristotle they were a necessity and that was all there was to it. But the ordinary theatre crowd had begun to put their minds on them with real discomfort, and Menander could write without fear of offense, "Think like a freeman and you will not be a slave." No early Southern playwright could have said that before our Civil War — or after it, either — and no Roman playwright ever. And again,

A slave that thinks great thoughts — that is a trouble.
A slave should not —

People were looking at their slaves as if they were human beings. In that little town alone in the whole world slavery was being questioned. The fact says much about the late fourth-century Athenians.

The picture Menander leaves us with is that of an

eminently civilized people. They are more than respectable; they are estimable, kindly, well-meaning, well-mannered. Their standards are high and their intelligence is excellent. They accept their loss of freedom quietly, without any ill-bred fussing, and are ready to make the best of what is left to them. Private property is safe; they can have what they want for comfort at home and they are able to put out of mind what they cannot have. After all, was political freedom ever very important to them? Before the Macedonians took it away from them they had willingly given up much of their independence. They had begun to rely more and more upon the state and less and less upon themselves. Independence is freedom's other name, and the people Menander wrote for were prepared by the time the garrison was installed to live contentedly without freedom.

This picture of the Athenians is of real importance for the reason that with the end of the fourth century, during the lifetime of Menander's audience, the greatness of Athens came to an end, and none of the other writers of the day show us so clearly why that was. From this point of view the entire fourth century is a puzzle. There is so much that is great in it: Plato and Aristotle, very gods; Isocrates and Demosthenes, giants of lofty stature; the shattering brief earthquake which was Alexander. The fourth century ought to be not only bright with a true glory, but a prelude to more

glory of great thought and great art. Instead, what follows that outburst of genius lofty as any the world has
known is Menander. The divine fire has burned out.
When Menander began to write, Plato and Isocrates
had been dead, the first nearly thirty, the second nearly
twenty, years; Aristotle had left the city; Demosthenes
was discredited; both died soon after. The men who
succeeded them were not — obviously as Menander
shows them to us — equal to their task. They had been
trained to high idealism. Their fathers had sat under
Plato; they themselves had listened to Aristotle and Isocrates and Demosthenes. They had started out eager to
serve their city. But they had had to face grim realities
— the loss of liberty, the end of the democracy, the
country in the hands of the Macedonians. And they
themselves had been educated in the school of comfortable dependence on the state. To such people such a task
would be appalling, not arousing.

The men who fought at Marathon and Salamis made
the Periclean age. A hundred and fifty years later their
descendants accepted the loss of what their forefathers
had won, and they are the characters in Menander's plays.

The decline of Rome was ushered in by moral de-
generacy. Not so the decline of Greece. There could be
nothing less like the blood-stained splendor of the early
Roman emperors than the audience Menander introduces
us to. Athens declined quietly and inconspicuously, in

a civilized way. She faded out, and Menander shows us why. His small men and women absorbed in small personal matters could not keep her greatness alive. For that there would have had to be fire of conviction, a flaring up of "the soul's invincible surmise," spiritual vigor and energy. But there was no fire. "A spark disturbs our clod." In these plays the spark is dead.

On an Egyptian tomb when the first dynasty was falling into ruins someone inscribed the words, "And no one is angry enough to speak out." None of Menander's stage people and none of his audience ever felt that kind of anger, white-hot at corruption and injustice. Only what touched them personally made them angry. A sudden breaking out of the spirit of Marathon is inconceivable in them. Ahead of them in history lay the Roman conquest and they were predestined to be its victims. As far as we can tell, Athens retired contentedly to the position of a university town. Her light of genius flickered up waveringly a few times and then died forever.

Chapter VIII

THE STOICS

Zeno and Epictetus

"THE TRUE nature of anything," Aristotle says, "is what it becomes at its highest." Not the embryo, but the full-grown man; not any man, but man at his greatest. Stoicism is a proof for Aristotle. It started in Greece in the early third century B.C., but it can be known in its true nature only in Rome in the second century A.D. There in the persons of two men, one a slave and one an emperor, it showed itself at its highest so that any account of it which was limited to its career in Greece would be so imperfect as to miss most of the truth. This Greek philosophy of the classical world must be studied chiefly in Rome when the classical world had ended.

The Greeks were notably disinclined to theology. Dogma did not interest them. The first really dogmatic teacher in Athens was the founder of Stoicism, Zeno. It was a religion first, a philosophy only second. Zeno was almost certainly not a Greek, but a Semite, of a practical bent therefore, not given naturally to theories and abstractions, inclined to estimate the truth in terms of what it did to men's lives rather than to their ways of thinking. When he came to Athens as a young merchant, one story says, bringing a cargo of Tyrian purple, the city was full of theories and abstractions. This was a few years after Aristotle's death. The Athenians had an ineradicable habit of using their minds, and when, with Macedon's conquest, politics became out of bounds for thinking men, they took to philosophy, which kept them occupied and was perfectly harmless from the Macedonian point of view. They had a host of schools to choose from: Plato's Academics were still with them and Aristotle's Peripatetics, and there were Pyrrhics and Cynics and Skeptics, Epicureans, too, a new school just started, and others besides. They all attacked each other joyously and discussed what the truth was endlessly.

It must all have been an amazement to the young Phoenician. Just what happened we do not know, beyond the fact that he found the atmosphere of the city so delightful he could not bear to leave her. He stayed there all his life and spent years in the schools studying with this man and that. It is said in one of the few stories that have come down about him that he had lived twenty years in Athens listening to other people talk before he finally began to talk himself. His favorite spot was a porch — *stoa* in Greek — where he spoke so often he became known as the Stoic.

The other philosophies of the day, except Plato's and Aristotle's, did not live very long. Only Stoicism endured. Five hundred years after Zeno a Roman emperor turned Stoic exemplified in his life Plato's philosopher-king, and during all the years in between, Stoicism produced men marked out by an extraordinary serenity and strength. They proved their doctrine by the way they lived and died.

Not much of Zeno's teaching has survived. We know what Stoicism is chiefly from his followers, but it is clear that he turned away from Plato and Aristotle. It has been well said of him that he wanted not to know, but to prove. Theory was not what he was searching for, but a definite and practical guide for a confused and frightened world. It is equally clear that he found one in Socrates, who had proved what he believed in the most practical way possible, by dying for it, and who had said to his judges, "No evil can happen to a good man either in life or after death." This saying is the very heart of Zeno's doctrine. It is difficult to conceive of anything less like Socrates than the inner aloofness and the contempt for life's amenities, not to say the stern austerity, which were strong tendencies in Stoicism; but the core of it came straight from Socrates, his impregnable security, his complete independence of all that could happen to him. Nothing evil could happen if he were doing God's business, as he put it. Socrates said, "Nothing which does not make a man worse can harm him." Therefore he was never afraid.

The people who listened to Zeno were afraid and very evil things were happening to them. It is true that there was still an élite minority, Menander's elegant, cultivated people, living in their comfortable houses and shutting their eyes to everything outside, but the great majority were in a state of confusion and fear, thrown off their base by events never dreamed of before by any Athenian. Their city, the only place in the world where they could look for any well-being, which had been the freest city and the proudest, had suddenly been cast down helpless. She could do nothing; she must submit to whichever of the war-lords — Alexander's generals — wanted to possess her. There was no freedom anywhere, no security, nothing a man could count on. The old gods were gone. Even Plato's and Isocrates' schoolboys had laughed at them. What did Plato's ideals mean? Nothing an ordinary man could hold to. And Aristotle's God serenely undisturbed by anything was certainly no present help in trouble. Athens had been the guiding star to her citizens; she had raised them to a level where they were ready to die for her. She had been their home, too, their safe, well-ordered, beautiful home. The star had set, the home was in ruins, and they saw no path to walk on.

These were the people Zeno spoke to when he said: There is nothing to fear. In all the world you need fear nothing and no one. You are free, you are safe, no harm can come to you. Do you ask how that can be when evil and pain and death are around you all the time? The answer is that none of these is of any importance to your real self, the self that is truly you. The only thing of importance is what you are and that is in your own power and in your power only. Nothing and no one can make you good or bad except yourself, and that is all that matters. To those Athenians this was a message of hope to the despairing, of liberty to the conquered, of courage and self-reliance.

Yet it was no easy way out. It was hard doctrine; nevertheless, it took hold of the people and it spread. That must be remembered in any estimation of the third-century Athenians. They are described as reluctant to make an effort, mental or physical, comfortably unheroic and wanting nothing adventurous, bent upon easy pleasures, but there was something else underneath, or Zeno would have failed. He preached nothing that was comfortable and easy, he made no concessions to human weakness. The standard he held up was impossibly high, but the Stoics never lowered it. ("Be ye perfect even as your Father in Heaven is perfect.")

Do you tell me, Zeno said in effect, that not only things and events are outside of you, but people, too, family, friends, fellow citizens. Do they, too, not matter? Only to the degree that you can help them. You must be ready to do everything for them, to sacrifice all that you have, your health, your life, even. You must always remember that all men are your brothers, down to the vilest and most debased; all are sons of the same heavenly father. They are your family and your friends. Your fellow-citizens as well, because the whole world is the City of God and whatever happens to the least of God's children happens to the others.

You must be kind, therefore, endlessly kind, "patient with all who suffer, not because of their outside troubles, but because of their inward blindness and weakness," a later Stoic says. "If you are wronged do not take it ill or be angry. The person really wronged is the man who wronged you. He had no power to do you harm. Only be anxious to make friends with him, to meet the least approach on his part. Any question of your personal honor is folly. No one can dishonor you."

But more than that you must not do. You must not admit anyone, his griefs and pains, to your inner citadel, where the one thing of importance is to will what God wills. To that stronghold grief and pain must never come. They will not if you have given up your will to God's will. Men have tried to get happiness by making outside things as they wanted them to be. They have never felt secure; they have always lived in fear of what might happen. But if God's will is your will, you will want whatever happens and you will never fear. "Is it God's will that I should have a fever?" one of the last Stoics, Epictetus, said. "Then it is my will too." Through everything that took place God was working out His purpose so that nothing outside a man could disturb him. And within he would be always at peace. ("The kingdom of God is within you.") There a Stoic would refuse to let suffering and sorrow enter.

"Show me a man who is sick and happy," a Stoic said, "who is in danger and happy, in disgrace and happy. Show me him — by Zeus, I am asking to be shown a Stoic." Epictetus, perhaps the greatest of the Stoics, was a slave to an official of Nero and doubly helpless in a court where the fortune of the greatest hung on an imperial scoundrel's whim — and he was happy. He was free, he said. "To obey God is liberty." He was able to do whatever he wanted; he was independent of whatever men could do to him. "Does the tyrant say he will throw me into prison? He cannot imprison my spirit. Does he say that he will put me to death? He can only cut off my head."

There is a suggestion here of life after death, but Epictetus never dealt directly with the subject. Zeno had expressed contempt for those who held out pleasures or pains in a future life as a motive for being good, and in general the Stoics followed him there. It was a Stoic who said, "Virtue is its own reward," and they seem to have wanted no other. But as regards immortality, the Stoic Seneca, who held an important post under Nero, wrote at some length about it, saying that this life is a prelude to a better and the body is only "a lodging place," words which were perhaps in the mind of the emperor Hadrian, no Stoic, as far as we know, when on his death bed he called his soul "the body's guest." The Stoic's sharp distinction between the outside and the inside carried with it inevitably the spirit's independence of the body and therefore of death.

Epictetus was freed, we do not know when or why, and he is said to have been among the philosophers banished by the emperor Domitian. He went to live in a little town in Epirus and many came to learn from him. He emphasized especially two ideas, latent in Stoicism but first clearly expressed by Seneca, the nearness of God to man and the happiness of doing His will. Seneca writes, "I do not obey God, I agree with Him." Zeno had said that the power behind all that is was good and met men in their endeavor to be good, but Seneca and Epictetus were conscious of a divine presence always with them, uplifting them and strengthening them. "When you go to your room and close the door,"

Seneca says, "do not think you are alone. God is there."
"Whatever post God entrusts me with," Epictetus says,
" 'I will die ten thousand times,' to quote Socrates, 'sooner
than abandon it'. Then if something men call undesirable
happens to me I will remember, it comes from outside
my will — how can it concern me? And then will come
the commanding question, Who sent it to me? And with
that the delight of knowing that I am obeying God. He
is showing me to men poor or sick or in prison not because He does not care for me — He cares for the
lowliest — but because He is training me to be a witness.
Then I give Thee all thanks that Thou has allowed me
to join the great company of mankind to see Thy works
and understand Thy ways. Let us sing hymns to God
and bless Him and tell of all His benefits."

It is often said that Stoicism was un-Greek, that it
suited Romans far better, and it is true that it had its
most distinguished and conspicuous success in Rome,
where it won over two men of genius, the slave and the
emperor. Nevertheless, the core of Stoicism was pure
Greek, not Roman at all. It was the ideal of self-mastery
which Greece first proclaimed, which she valued most,
and which guided her in all of good that she achieved,
in government, in art, in thought. That was not a Roman
ideal; Rome valued most obedience to authority. The
Stoics did not look back to the Semitic Zeno, but to the
Greek Socrates. There are many times as many refer-

ences to him as there are to Zeno. He was their model.
"If you are not Socrates," Epictetus says, "live as one
who wants to become Socrates," and he bids his students
— thereby displaying his critical acumen — "Read Socrates with the spirit of Socrates and not as just so much
Isocrates." Marcus Aurelius, too, quotes him often,
though by nature he had little in common with Socrates.
Stoicism never became really Romanized in spite of the
great Romans who adopted it.

There is even something essentially Greek in Stoic
austerity, remote as that seems from Periclean Athens.
It was not like any other kind of austerity. There was
nothing in excess. The body was not to be mortified or
punished or weakened. The Stoic did not hate it, he
was indifferent to it. Undoubtedly it was hardened and
made more fit by the way he lived, but that was not his
object. He lived simply and plainly because outside
pleasures meant nothing to him. He was not given to
fasting and the idea of self-chastisement never entered
his mind. Greek moderation was always present. The
ecstasies of self-torture which later ages developed had
their origin in Rome, not in Greece. Zeno lived with
the utmost simplicity — he would not have even one
slave to work for him — but it is on record that he said
beans soaked in wine were very good.

The words bring to mind Him who "came eating
and drinking." Stoic sayings again and again recall

Christ's teachings. He too preached a hard doctrine and disregarded nonessentials. When He told the Samaritan woman, "Ye shall neither in this mountain, nor yet at Jerusalem, worship the Father. God is a spirit and they that worship him must worship him in spirit and in truth," He was disregarding the whole apparatus of outside worship. He was indifferent to it. Zeno could not reach that height; he must denounce it. Zeno was opposed to temples; Christ thought they did not matter. But Christ would have approved Zeno's conception of God, "Who dwelleth not in temples made with hands," and when He said, "A man's life consisteth not in the abundance of the things which he possesseth," he was uttering one of Zeno's dearest truths. The fundamental Stoic ideal, independence of whatever happens, was a Christian ideal, too, but here the two separated. Christianity parted sharply from Stoicism in its idea of what independence was.

When St. Paul wrote, "And though I bestow all my goods to feed the poor, and though I give my body to be burned, and have not love it profiteth me nothing," he was not trying to add to the ideal of Stoic benevolence, which embraced all the world; he was directly opposing their most cherished ideal, he was admitting love to the innermost citadel and thereby pain. St. Paul knew well that love is indissolubly joined to pain: "Love beareth all things, believeth all things, hopeth all things, endureth all things." Christian peace did not exclude pain. Both were present at Gethsemane.

Marcus Aurelius

The last Stoic we know of was an extremely conspicuous person. This religion of rejecting life's pleasures; of detachment from all that men seek and have sought and will forever seek, power, honor, ease, applause; a religion of wanting with a single-hearted devotion one thing only, to be and to do good; a religion of supreme self-denial — this was embraced by a Roman emperor. It does not need a moment's thought to realize how extraordinary this was. The ruler of the world — the civilized world and a good deal of the uncivilized — all that men seek was his, everything desirable that was to be had, every pleasure man has ever thought of. He had but to lift his finger and hundreds would try to bring him or do for him what he wanted. And with the world at his feet ready to give him everything, he chose a religion which bade him turn away from all the world had to give. He became a Stoic, a man who wanted nothing. Not enough has been made of this astonishing event. It has been little commented on. Still, it is true that all comment on him has been very generally favorable. No one has ever attacked him to pull down his character. It would seem that his goodness and disinterestedness were so great and so manifest that would-be detractors were discouraged.

And yet he seems not to have received his due. His name is known everywhere, but not much more than that. He is a dim far-away figure about whom no stories are told nor ballads written to bring him to life. A great man unquestionably, but not a popular great man. Nor is he enrolled in the company of the saints, which seems his natural place. Certainly none of them lived a life sterner to himself and gentler to others. The saints are the brotherhood to which he belongs except in two respects. The joy which was a marked characteristic of so many of them he had none of. He met life with enduring courage and unfailing sweetness, but always sadly. And he was unlike most of the saints in turning away from the solitary life he longed for and staying in the world of affairs which he hated. But in the matter of importance, sheer goodness, he was truly a saint.

He was the Emperor Antoninus' nephew, and after his uncle's death in 161 A.D. he became emperor. Long before that he had had a prominent part in administering the state, and for nineteen years he ruled alone except for a worthless adopted son of the emperor's whom he associated with himself, but who fortunately died early. During these years the barbarians began to attack the northern frontier, and he spent many months in fighting them. He detested war and all that has to do with it, and apparently nothing would have been easier than to turn the whole business over to some general, but to choose the easier part anywhere would have been to him a betrayal of the faith.

We know his attitude not from the report of others, but from himself. He left a book of meditations — *Things Addressed to Himself*, he calls it — which is really a collection of little sermons preached to himself when he felt especially alone and must collect all his inner forces to keep on the road he had chosen. He attaches to two of them the places where he wrote them on the Danube when he was fighting; where the others were written we are not told, but in every one he is a man all alone, facing the everlasting fact by himself.

In this book, obviously written to reach no one's eyes except his own, he can be seen, of course, as very few of history's generally nonvocal characters can be, but unfortunately it is not a book of confessions. We cannot know Marcus Aurelius as we know St. Augustine. It is a book of exhortations. We are left with the impression that the author was not interested in himself except in the one matter of being and doing good. There is not a suggestion of anything like St. Augustine's lively account of his sins and his passion of penitence. Marcus Aurelius is not concerned with the past except to review gratefully all the blessings God has given him — "Nearly everything good," he writes.

The fact that he is the emperor never comes into
the book unless perhaps there is just a hint when he says,
"Must a man live in a palace? Well, then, he can live well
in a palace." His truly terrific power and supreme emi-
nence never enter his mind, at least, he never so much as
hints at them, when he tries to outline for himself what
his life should be. It cannot be doubted that in the final
analysis they were not important to him. He seems indeed raised to the superhuman Stoic ideal, indifferent
to whatever happened to him, a man not entangled with
any personal considerations, and disinterested to a degree which has been paralleled only two or three times
in history.

He tells himself over and over again in any choice
presented to him, "Prefer the hard." This holds good not
only in great matters, but also in very small, in fighting
by the frozen Danube and in starting the day early. He
carried an immense burden of affairs and of course was
often a very tired man, and he writes more than once
how hard it is to begin the day "In the morning when you
get up so unwillingly." When he refused himself this
little lazy pleasure he wanted, never a thought that he
was emperor entered his mind, except as a cold reminder
that an emperor could not be late for business. In point
of fact, as he saw matters, an emperor could never do
what he wanted to do. "Cast away your thirst for
books," he tells himself. And again, "Stay in Rome though

you want very much a house by the sea or in the hills, a quiet retreat, a poor desire on your part, for you can always find a retreat within yourself. Retire into this place of your own and be free." But the lover of the sea and the mountains, although he could keep his body in the city, in the palace, had to struggle to keep his spirit there. He speaks almost violently about "your imagination which is not under your control. It bites deep into your soul. Do not suffer it to call up what pleasures it will." That is, in a palace where one can never be alone do not let yourself even think of an untrodden shore of the sea, a deep valley where no road runs. "Wipe out imagination," he says. And again, "What are you doing here, imagination? Go away. I do not want you. But you are always coming. I am not angry with you, but go away."

Along with this can be placed a few sentences about his love for doing what he calls "fine writing, rhetoric and poetry." He is grateful to those who turned him away from that sort of thing. He was only seventeen when a share in managing the empire was laid on his shoulders. Henceforward fine writing would inevitably appear the merest trifle. A love of writing poetry, no matter how great, could not survive under such circumstances, certainly not in a young man of his disposition, but the fact makes it easier to understand his repugnance to the whole mass of public business and his great long-

ing to be alone. He was not designed by nature to be the
emperor of the world, but in actual fact he was the best
of what are known as the five good emperors, of which
the judgment of history is that the world has never had
better rulers. His own idea of what government should
be he states once briefly: "A kingly government which
respects most of all the freedom of the governed."

And yet the Christians were almost certainly perse-
cuted during his reign. This is denied, of course, but
there seems more to be said in support of the statement
than against it. Nevertheless, the opinion of the world
generally has absolved him. The other persecuting emperors have come down to us as monsters, but no one,
no fiercest fanatic, could so represent this persecutor. On
the contrary, we are told how impossible it was that in
those days he could look at the Christians except as a
pernicious secret society creeping underground to sub-
vert the state. He was informed that it had been discovered at work in far-distant France, an alarming development. The officials asked for full authority to put
it down, which he gave them, and this, the best known,
was not the only time. Once he gives the Christians a
passing mention as influenced by "mere obstinacy." It is
only reasonable to conclude that he knew nothing of
what Christianity was. The record of his whole life
shows that he never judged severely or punished gladly.
One of the very few stories we have of him tells of his

marching to put down a claimant to the throne and saying when he was informed of his assassination that he was sorry to be deprived of the pleasure of pardoning him. He felt himself in very truth the brother of everyone, the evil as much as the good. "So close is the kinship between a man and the whole human race," he writes. "Love men. Follow God." But this disposition did not come easily to him. He did not naturally suffer fools gladly. Once he writes, "It is hardly possible to endure the pleasantest of those who live with you — to say nothing of a man's being hardly able to endure himself."

Still, he could always be kind. "Show gentleness," he says, "to those who try to hinder you. . . . We should blame nobody. . . . Feel kindness even to liars and evil men." Such sentences recur constantly. "Show good humor," he writes, "and do not look proud." When he walked through the palace in his magnificent imperial robes with every courtier's eye upon him he would be saying to himself, "You are just the same as all these people. Don't put on airs." But was there ever in all the world since the Pharaohs began another ruler like that? It can be more than doubted. Certainly we have no record of one.

As one reads and rereads the little book and tries to make a picture of what the writer, this most singular emperor, was like, one feels that those who lived with

him no matter how drawn to him by his beautiful goodness, must always have felt a great gulf between them
and him. It would seem that he too was conscious of
the fact. "When you are dying," he writes, "think, even
those I live with and have so cared for want me to depart, hoping to get some little advantage from it. But
do not, therefore, go away less kindly disposed to them."
He realized his own separateness. Living together happily
means giving and taking and there could be no question
of anyone's ever giving to Marcus Aurelius.

At this point his deplorable son Commodus comes
to mind. History has nothing good to say of him. He
turned violently away from everything his father stood
for. Astonishing folly and astonishing wickedness distinguished him, and the historians generally conclude
that Marcus Aurelius was a weak and overindulgent
father. Against this judgment all the rest of his life cries
out. He was not weak, but it is true that undeviating
loftiness of spirit can be difficult to live with. A soft
answer does not always turn away wrath; a succession
of them to an angry man can be highly exasperating.
Commodus would have had to be an uncommonly well-
balanced lad not to develop something of an inferiority
complex and be driven to try to assert himself in his
father's presence. And always it was a failure; always
he was received with serene kindness no matter what
he did. He could not even make his father angry. He

was by no means a well-balanced lad, and he was all prepared for a violent revolt against every kind of superiority when he became emperor. It had been, of course,
impossible for his father ever to admit him even for a
moment to his inner citadel of perfect peace. Christ
loved one of his disciples beyond the others; he wept
when he heard of Lazarus' death. Marcus Aurelius was
always immovably aloof.

Aloofness means loneliness. He was a very lonely
man, longing for companionship and never finding it.
The prevailing tone of his book is sad. "Life is a warfare. . . . Life is a stranger's sojourn." He is constantly
making statements like that. And on nearly every page
in one form or another he bids himself, "practice tolerance and self-restraint and remember everything else is
not yours nor in your power."

Did he ever seriously consider all the things that
were factually in his power? The evidence is overwhelm-
ing that none of them represented any value to him; in
his eyes they had no real existence. "Death and life," he
says, "honor and dishonor, pain and pleasure, make us
no better and no worse and so they are neither good nor
bad." A man is enabled to know this truth and thereby
become absolutely free by "the divine spirit planted
within him."

This is the last voice of Stoicism. It is so elevated, so
extraordinarily noble, that its apparent passing away

after Marcus Aurelius' death seems to contradict Aristotle's assertion that the excellent becomes the permanent. But the truth is that it did not pass away. It lived on in the great system of Roman Law which followed Stoicism when it took as its basis the nature of man, not the classes of society. And when the first Christian preacher in Athens spoke to "certain philosophers of the Epicureans and of the Stoics," what he said was in chief a statement of the Stoic creed: "God that made the world and all things therein dwelleth not in temples made with hands. Who hath made of one blood all nations of men for to dwell on all the face of the earth, that they should seek the Lord, if haply they might find him, though he be not far from every one of us; for in him we live and move and have our being." Through Paul, who was of Tarsus where the Stoics had a great school, Stoicism also lived on. It merged into Christianity with little difficulty. An early Stoic wrote, "They who turn to God He hardens," and in those days Christianity too was a hard religion. A Christian was expected to give up much and to live dangerously. The Stoics found it congenial. They had by then turned away from most of their theology, always the separating factor in religions, and in their fundamental belief they had much akin to Him who said: Be of good cheer: I have overcome the world.

Chapter IX

PLUTARCH

In the eleventh century of our era a bishop of the Byzantine Church made a prayer: "If, Lord, thou art willing in thy grace to save any Pagans from the wrath of God, I pray thee humbly to save Plato and Plutarch." They were such truly good men, he said, and he gave the Lord to understand that he cared so much for them, he could not bear to have them lost forever.

That was some nine hundred years after Plutarch's death, and in the nine hundred years since, the bishop's opinion has never been challenged, only endorsed many times over down the ages. That prayer strikes the dominant note in all the tributes that have been paid to Plutarch. It is the note of personal affection, not often heard when a man's writing is appraised. Most good writers are admired; only a very few are loved. Who ever dreamed of feeling affection for Gibbon, or, for that matter, Thucydides or Tacitus? Who loves Stendhal or Flaubert or Proust or Henry James or Steinbeck or Hemingway? All these have seen in a very great degree men's misery and meanness and spiritual poverty; in some degree their pitifulness; but they have not seen them as lovable, they do not even like them. But there are writers who love mankind and in return mankind loves them. There is no other open sesame to that particular response on the part of readers. The bishop had a sure instinct, Plato possesses it as well as Plutarch. Horace stands with them. It is a mixed company. Chaucer belongs to it and Scott and Dickens and Burns and Charles Lamb and Trollope. Sir Thomas Browne, also, who always has a circle, small but very select, of true lovers. Anyone can fill out the list, but there is hardly a better guarantee of immortality than to be on it, and no one has a more assured place there than Plutarch. Only the other day a distinguished Greek scholar called him "the most widely beloved of all the literary treasures of Greece."

He was born a few years after the death of Christ, around the year 45, and he lived into the next century. Those fifty or sixty years are immensely important. They saw the entry into the world of the Christian Church. During them the Gospels were coming into existence and the new society was taking shape. When we think of the first century after Christ's death we are apt to see it dramatically. Two figures only engage our attention, the pure and radiant earliest Church of Christ

and the Rome of Nero and Caligula. It is a strikingly
dramatic contrast. On the one side are the Gospels and
St. Paul's Epistles and the existence they point to of a
society founded in purity and charity and faith, and on
the other side accounts of cruelty and vice which have
never been surpassed and seldom equaled in the long
annals of history. On the stage of the world lofty goodness confronts atrocious wickedness.

The page of history thus unrolled looks, of course,
very attractive, all in vivid colors or clearest blacks and
whites, no dullness anywhere, no half-tones. The greatest writers of that period did not admit such. St. Paul
did not see a gray world, nor yet the Roman writers who
have left a record of the age. The two greatest, Tacitus
and Juvenal, saw mankind sunk in an abyss of degradation, governed by tyrants run mad, and themselves given
up to hideous cruelty as shown in the amphitheater, and
monstrous vice as typified in Messalina. "An era of atroc-
ities," Tacitus calls it. "Nothing but base servility and a
deluge of blood shed by a despot in the hour of peace."
Those whose dearest had just been put to death would
"hasten to print kisses on the emperor's hand."

Juvenal was in full agreement. His world was a night-
mare city where no one could drink a cup of wine without fearing poison, where "every street is thronged with
gloomy-faced debauchees," and "never a one that does
not have its Clytemnestra," where banquets celebrate

unnatural and incestuous vice and spies abound "whose gentle whisper cuts men's throats."

The tragic power of Tacitus and Juvenal's blazing indignation and terrific vigor of expression have made this the familiar, one might say the popular, picture of the Roman world where the young Christian Church was beginning to live. It was endorsed to the full by the only contemporary Christian writer who treated the subject. This is the author of the Book of Revelation, a most singular document, as unclassical as a document could well be, but in the author's Hebrew fashion, poles apart from the Latin fashion, he backed Tacitus and Juvenal with his own peculiar power of violent invective. He sees "that great city which reigneth over the kings of the earth and sitteth upon seven hills," as "the habitation of devils and of every foul spirit and a cage of every unclean and hateful bird," "full of the filthiness of her fornication." The book is written with a kind of somber grandeur which has ensured the long life of its contribution to the picture of the first century of the Roman Empire. "A black and shameful age," is Tacitus' summary, and deeply underlined as it is by Juvenal and Revelation it has been generally assented to by historians, especially Church historians. The triumph of Christianity over this blackness and shame has been celebrated by many writers.

To this sink of iniquity, this vilest city of Rome,

during the reign of one of the worst of the emperors, Domitian, a young Greek came. His name was Plutarch and his home was a little town in Boeotia, Chaeronea, about halfway between Athens and Delphi. He was sent to Rome, he tells us, on public business, but one of his purposes while there was to give a series of lectures on philosophy, although he was obliged to deliver them in Greek because he had little Latin. This matter-of-fact statement comes to the reader with a shock of surprise. Where did he get his hearers? From among Tacitus' servile flatterers or Juvenal's gloomy-faced debauchees, to say nothing of the foul and unclean creatures of the Biblical writer? The pursuit of philosophy is hardly compatible with such characters, and certainly to lecture to them would seem not only a most unprofitable business, but dangerous as well. Indeed, one would suppose that no foreigner would willingly put himself in the power of such people for even a single day.

But all this portentous picture vanishes when Plutarch appears. He saw the city so differently that there seems no connection between his Rome and the black abode of crime and vice familiar to us. To him she was "the fairest of all the works of mankind," for all the peoples of the earth "an anchorage from the wandering seas," giving stability to a world which had never known it before. "For there now reigns among us a great peace and calm. Wars have ceased. Expulsions, seditions, tyrannies, are no more" — since Rome is Queen of the World. He also found the city "given to the liberal arts, where there are plenty of books and plenty of people who can remember what has escaped the pens of writers," pleasant, cultivated people who liked to tell him stories which had been handed down in their families about Caesar and Brutus and Mark Antony, and liked to listen to philosophy too. In Rome Plutarch lectured and studied and talked at his ease, living happily the student's life and the life of the man of the world.

One cannot but wonder if his writings ever fell into Tacitus' or Juvenal's hands. They were certainly in Rome when Plutarch gave the lectures. Possibly they met, the tragic historian, the bitter satirist, and the Greek to whom the world was a place full of interest and men generally likable and often admirable.

The contrast in the points of view is great. There is a good deal of contemporary backing for Tacitus and Juvenal. The Roman writers of the period were not optimists. But what the Greeks thought is very generally passed over. Plutarch is the only well-known Greek writer of that day and he is known chiefly as the author of the *Lives*. He has left us, however, a great deal besides, many writings which give an excellent idea of what he himself was like and his circle of friends and his home, and so what the Greeks of the day were like and the Greek point of view, an important matter for a true picture of the age. Plutarch was no eccentric genius. He was a steady-thinking, sober-minded man, obviously qualified to represent his countrymen. The reason that Greece saw things so differently from the great Latins was due to a fundamental difference in the way the two countries looked at life. Reality was for the most part unpleasant to the Romans and pleasant to the Greeks. The Greek way and the Roman way came together only rarely, and that is an important fact in understanding this important period. The two great influences in the Western world, the Greek and the Roman, were at many points antagonistic, and the time was at hand when the Christian Church would inevitably choose between them.

About Plutarch himself, what kind of man he was, we know much, but about his life only a little. He was born, as has been said, in the year, or near the year, 45 A.D. and he died certainly after 106, for he speaks of Trajan's spending that winter on the Danube. The date of his death is usually assumed to be 119 or 120, but nothing that he did or that happened to him can be dated with complete accuracy.

He was born in Chaeronea where his family were well-considered people, and except for a time of study in Athens and one or perhaps two journeys abroad he spent his life there, going, however, often to Delphi, as he was attached to the oracle in some official capacity. He seems to have had a singularly peaceful and pleasant life, spent with an affectionate family and many friends, cultivated, traveled men, as we see them in his dialogues.

A letter we have to his wife when their little daughter died while he was away shows a genuine love for her, and he speaks often and warmly of his two brothers. He speaks also of his "numerous children," but the exact number we do not know. The little girl who died seems to have been his only daughter.

He quotes both his grandfather and his great-grandfather in the *Life of Antony*. One can deduce with some reason that he grew up in a household where the atmosphere was not provincial, where good talk went on and the affairs of the great world claimed attention. A story he tells about his father shows that he was a man who understood human nature. "I remember," he says, "that when I was still young I was sent with a companion on a deputation to the pro-consul [the Roman governor]. My comrade was unable to go on and I performed the commission alone. When I returned and was about to give an account of what had been done, my father bade me privately to be careful not to say *I* went, or *I* said, but *we* went and *we* said. In all my account I must give a full share to my companion." The father seems to have bequeathed his wisdom to the son. In a most difficult age Plutarch lived a pleasant life and died a peaceful death, the latter as striking proof in those violent times as could be given of ability to get on with people.

He had, of course, extraordinary abilities, but they were not such as in a happier age would have turned him naturally to books. If he had been able to choose his manner of life he would have disregarded the artist that was in him and gone into active affairs. Great writer though he was, his bent was strongly practical. He said of himself that he "did not so much understand matters through words as words through experience and knowledge of matters."

The *Lives* as they have come down to us have been changed from their original form. As Plutarch planned the work, it was to consist of a series of parallels, one Greek life and one Roman, followed by a comparison, but in our collection the comparison is lacking in a number of cases. Several single lives, too, have been added. Also, some of the parallels have been lost. In the long lapse of time, however, between Plutarch's day and ours, the wonder is that so much has been preserved, another proof of his great popularity.

The rest of his writings are grouped under the general title of *Moralia*, but they are so unlike that no common name is appropriate. They are a collection of essays and letters and dialogues on most diverse subjects. The majority have to do with philosophy and ethics and religion, but they deal also with education and music and politics and archaeology and history and literature and mathematics and astronomy, and many other matters besides. Plutarch had an astonishing amount of information and almost everything in the world interested him. So he writes on Platonic Questions, and the Training of Children, and the First Principle of Cold, and the Three Sorts of Government, and the Virtues of Women, and Whether it is Good Manners to Talk Philosophy at Table (at his own table, he says, questions on history and poetry are always the second course) and Why Mushrooms are Produced by Thunder, and What God is Worshiped by the Jews, and Why Women Do Not Eat the Middle Part of a Lettuce — the list is encyclopedic. Socrates once told the young Theaetetus that to wonder was a very philosophic attitude of mind, and in that sense no one was ever a better philosopher than Plutarch.

His private life was eminently successful. Nothing emerges so clearly from his writings as his own sweet and kindly temper of mind. He knew how to create happiness around him, and the fact is a great tribute to him, for most men, even of far less ability than he, would have been dissatisfied and embittered and a trial to live with. A successful public life was impossible for Plutarch, as for any Greek of the day. Greece was a humiliated, conquered country, largely depopulated, desperately poor, commerce gone, agriculture in hardly better case, more shepherds than farmers on the land. A traveler in Greece, Pausanias, a few years after Plutarch's death, saw "shrunken or ruined cities, deserted villages, roofless temples . . . faint vestiges of places which had once played a part in history."

Rome treated the country fairly well. The Greeks had some measure of self-government; their education, their courts of law, were not interfered with. But over all was the Roman governor with full power to interfere if he chose, and Rome's taxation, tribute, it was called, from the conquered to the conqueror, could be crushing when an emperor needed money. The Roman idea of civilization, a world brought together by great laws and great roads, meant nothing to Greece. She was too poor to keep roads in repair and she had her own great system of law. That was the world Plutarch was born into. He says of his own province Boeotia, where once great Thebes had flourished, "She is mute, altogether desolate and forlorn," and he calls his native town, "a poor little place, where I remained willingly so that it should not become even less." We have a letter of his to a young friend urging him to enter public life to the degree open to a Greek, which throws a light on the way he looked at himself. He tells him, "You will have no wars to wage, no tyrants to put down, no alliances to consolidate. The utmost you can hope for is to abolish some petty abuse, fight some bad custom, revive some charitable foundation, repair an aqueduct, rebuild a temple, adjust a local tax." They are all duties well worth doing, he tells his friend.

There is sadness in the words coming from a man who must have been aware of great powers in himself, and there is a wonderful high courage too. Plutarch did just what he advised. He threw himself into the petty details of small-town management, business of little moment and less interest. He said of himself that his neighbors often laughed at him when they saw him watching, for instance, while stone and mortar were measured out, but he would only say, "This is done not for myself, but for my country." That was the way he spent his life, "centered in the sphere of little things," but never despising them and never pitying himself. There is something here, some feeling, some ideal, which was not in Periclean Athens. Suffering may teach a profound lesson, and the mighty Greek spirit which had suffered so much had not lost its power to learn and to perceive new forms of excellence. When Plutarch declared that he who is faithful in that which is least may be fulfilling life's highest demands, he was Greece's far-sighted spokesman for a change that was beginning in the moral atmosphere of the world.

This conviction kept him from seeking a field fitted to his powers, in Rome, in Alexandria. He would stay in his own sorely stricken country and let nothing pass him

that could help her. But his thoughts were not limited
to one poor little town. He could send them where he
pleased, soaring away with those who had not had to
be content with humble duties in a lowly place, with
men who had molded the world to their desires. Within
that careful, patient guardian of Chaeronea's buildings
and taxes and water supply there dwelt a passionate lover
of great deeds, of heroic courage and splendid generosity, of magnificence in life and majesty in death. That
was what turned Plutarch into a writer. He could not be
an Aristides to lift Greece up by great statesmanship,
or an Alexander to make her the mistress of the world.
The time was long since over when a Greek could lead
states or armies. But the time was never over for trying
to help men to a loftier view of what it means to be a
man. The mighty dead could teach that lesson. So Plutarch set himself to write his Lives. "It was for the sake
of others," he says, "that I first began to write biogra-
phies, but I find myself continuing to do it for my own.
The virtues of these great men serve me as a sort of
looking-glass in which I may see how to adorn and adjust my own life. I can compare it to nothing but living daily with them ... turning my thoughts happily
and calmly to the noble."

Yet it cannot be said of him that he did not understand human nature and saw mankind far too favorably.
It is true that he kept always the quality of mercy. Even

Nero he would have spend only a short time in purgatory and then be given another chance, but he looked straight at the evil in men and he was perfectly aware that not one was righteous. In one essay he says, "If you will scrutinize and open up yourself you will find a storehouse of evils and maladies, not entering from abroad, but homebred, springing from vice, plenteous in passions. Wickedness frames the engines of her own torment. She is a wonderful artisan of a miserable life."

As a historian he has been drastically criticized for his romantic turn of mind; indeed, he is usually dismissed with a smile from the historians' domain as a mere storyteller. That is to do him an injustice. He was a first-rate storyteller, but his aim was not to please but to tell the truth, and he had a real power of critical judgment. In his lives of semi-mythical heroes like Theseus, Lycurgus, Romulus, and Numa, he is perfectly aware that his sources are "full of suspicion and doubt, being only poets and inventors of fables," and he asks his readers to "receive with indulgence the stories of antiquity." "So very difficult is it," he says, "to find out the truth of anything." He rejects all the marvelous tales reported of Alexander's death, which include one of his being poisoned by a deadly water cold as ice, distilling from a rock and kept in an ass's hoof "because it was so very cold and penetrating no other vessel would hold it." All such stories, he declares, are the inventions of writers who tried "to make the last scene of so great an action as tragical and moving as they could." Plutarch will have none of them. He gives word for word the meager and factual account in the court journal of the time, an undramatic record of a fever which increased for ten days and then proved fatal.

He did love those who could use life for grand purposes and depart from it as grandly, but he would not pass over weaknesses and vices which marred the grandeur. His hero of heroes is Alexander the Great; he loves him above all other men, while his abomination of abominations is bad faith, dishonorable action. Nevertheless he tells with no attempt to extenuate how Alexander promised a safe conduct to a brave Persian army if they surrendered, and then, "even as they were marching away he fell upon them and put them all to the sword," "a breach of his word," Plutarch says sadly, "which is a lasting blemish to his achievements." He adds piteously, "but the only one — ." He hated to tell that story.

His aim was the truth, not brightly colored romances; but historic truth and artistic truth are not the same and Plutarch was an artist. He says that his purpose is to write lives, not histories, and he had a clear idea what the difference between the two was. A Life was a portrait, which Socrates once told a great painter must be a portrayal of the man's inner self, a revelation of what he really was. A History was an account of men's actions and fortunes irrespective of what the people were like who produced them. Economics and politics and the rise and fall of empires were the historian's concern; the biographer's was human beings. The two could not use the same methods. "The most glorious exploits," Plutarch says, "do not always furnish the clearest indications of virtue or vice in men; sometimes a mere expression, a jest, even, gives us their characters better than the most famous sieges, the bloodiest battles." These are history's material, but for himself, "I must be allowed to give my particular attention to the marks and indications of men's souls, as I endeavor to portray their lives."

In one passage he likens himself to a painter aware of an imperfection in the face he is painting, aware too that he must not leave it out, but above all that if he stresses it the likeness will be lost. So, he continues, he will follow the truth exactly in that which is excellent, but "not introduce faults officiously, if it be but out of tenderness for the weakness of human nature."

Debunking was odious to him, of course. The sharpest censure he was capable of was given to a writer who tried to pull a great man down from his pedestal. One such who had attacked the unfortunate general Nicias, forced against his will to lead the disastrous expedition to Sicily, was only trying, Plutarch says, to make himself out a better historian than Thucydides, "and," he remarks coldly, "only succeeded in showing himself half-lettered and childish, accurately described in Pindar's lines,

> "One who on his feet
> "Would with Lydian cars compete."

Then he permits himself a little sarcasm, a weapon he rarely used: "This may be merely another indication of the admirable taste which makes him abuse Plato and Aristotle."

"I myself," Plutarch declares, "will briefly recount the errors and faults of Nicias, because they illustrate his character under his many and great troubles." Also he will add to his biography "matters not commonly known, but found in old archives and on old monuments, not in order to collect useless bits of learning, but only those that make his disposition understood."

The deep seriousness which he brought to his work was founded on his religion, or, as he would have put it, on his philosophy. His profoundest conviction was that we needs must love the highest when we see it — but who can see it if there are none to show it, first, of course, in their lives, but, second only to that, in their words? The one he raised to a pedestal was the man who made it easy for people to believe in goodness and greatness, in heroic courage and warm generosity and lofty magnanimity. In humble virtues, too, patience that never wearies; readiness to forgive; kindness to an erring servant, to an animal. Plutarch was the first man to write about treating animals kindly. Below, far below such men stood the biographer, but the task of the latter was a high obligation none the less, since virtue unheralded must quickly be forgotten. "We are right," he says, "to blame those who misuse the natural love of inquiry and observation by expending it on unworthy objects. Every man is able to turn his mind easily upon what he thinks good. It is a duty to contemplate the best." St. Paul never came Plutarch's way — he seems not to have had any contact with Christianity — but if he had known him Plutarch would have endorsed with all his heart, "Whatsoever things are true, whatsoever things are pure, whatsoever things are lovely, if there be any virtue and if there be any praise, think on these things."

As a Greek, Plutarch had for his birthright the belief that men had within them "the mysterious preference for the best," and that they could strengthen it or weaken it, and he knew his own obligation. "Admirable actions," he writes, "can produce, even in the minds of those who only read about them, an eagerness which may lead them to imitate them. He who busies himself in mean occupations is his own evidence that he does not care for what is really good. The bare account of noble deeds can make us admire and long to follow the doers of them. Moral good is a practical stimulus; it is no sooner seen than it inspires an impulse to follow it."

In all this Plutarch was the true representative of Greece. Plato was at his most Greek when he said that to describe the ugliness and weakness of men was to give only the appearance, not the truth, and that men's supreme duty was to trace out the examples — the forms — of excellence, which would enable them to choose the right pattern for their lives.

Plutarch's Lives is essentially a book of such patterns, models on which men may mold themselves, and, above all, be inspired to do so. What has made the book live for 1800 years is that Plutarch's spirit breathes through it and sweeps the reader along, a glowing sense of how great and how good greatness and goodness are, how wonderful human beings can be, how admirable are courage and the disdain of death and the high sense of honor and the contempt of the petty and the mean. Greatness is Plutarch's theme, not great fortune — he loves to depict a hero in adversity: "The truly noble and resolved spirit becomes more evident in times of disaster"; not great power, which he distrusts and disapproves: "Such an unsociable solitary thing is power"; but great character: "Those who are great produce nothing little." Plato had said that men built on a grand scale sometimes stand forth because of the magnitude of their vices, not their virtues, and Plutarch's villains along with his heroes scorn the mean and what Schiller called, "Das was uns alle bändigt, das Gemeine." To such a villain he always gives full credit for any good in him. He says of Alcibiades, whom he really detested for his arrogance and treachery, "He had such pleasant comely ways, he won over everybody. The charm of daily intercourse with him was more than any could resist."

Antony was the cause of terrible evils and Plutarch does not minimize a single one, but in the worst action of all his life he shows him to be pitied. At Actium when Cleopatra fled, Antony, "as if he had been part of her and must move wheresoever she went, abandoned those that were fighting and spending their lives for him, to follow her. She as he reached her fleet took him into her own ship. But without looking at her he went forward by himself to the prow and sat him down alone, covering his face with his hands, and there he remained for three days." This passage is an example of Plutarch's power to convey the significance of what is happening without a single comment. No one needs to have put into words what went on in Antony's mind as he sat there.

This is the literature of aristocracy. It belongs with the *Morte d' Arthur*. The grand manner is always there, in death as in life. Caesar's lieutenant, captured and offered his life, answers, "Caesar's soldiers give, but do not take, mercy," and he falls on his sword. Alexander, choked with thirst in a battle in the desert and offered a helmet full of water, refuses it because his soldiers need

it as much as he. His enemy, Darius, dying on the field
and given a cup of water by a Roman, says when he has
quenched his thirst that the last extremity of his ill fortune is to receive a kindness and not be able to return
it. Chivalry was first born in Plutarch's pages. When
Alexander captures Darius' camp with his mother and
wife and daughters, Arthur himself could not have improved upon his behavior. He is a forerunner of Lance-
lot when, urged to attack the Persian army under the
cover of night, he cries, "I will not steal a victory."

Prudence and common sense are of course most
useful and highly to be commended, but how delightful
and thrilling it can be when they are splendidly dismissed by those who are willing to pay for the dismissal
with their lives. Pyrrhus was near to conquering the
Romans. His physician sent the Roman commander a
letter in which he offered to poison Pyrrhus and so end
the war. The Roman sent this letter to Pyrrhus and
wrote him, "You are fighting honorable men who will
not conquer by treachery." The Athenians during a
fierce contest with Philip of Macedon surprised a mes-
senger of his with letters. They opened them, except
those to his wife which they returned to him with the
seals intact. "The grace and the gentleness of true greatness," Plutarch remarks. Pompey, despatched to Africa by
the senate to bring back a shipload of corn with all speed
to hungry Rome, upon being told by the sailors when the

ship was loaded that they could not set sail in such a storm, cried, "There is a necessity upon us to sail. There is no necessity upon us to live."

Such stories fill Plutarch's pages and make an appeal to some disdain within us all of the man who loves life most, some sense of pride as well that human beings have been like that, since we too are human.

Our own greatest stories are built on Plutarch's model. The Charge of the Light Brigade is pure Plutarch.

> Was there a man dismayed?
> Not though the soldiers knew
> Some one had blundered.

In other words, "There is no necessity upon us to live." Sir Richard Grenville, engaging the entire Spanish fleet with the little *Revenge*, belongs to Plutarch's company and he dies like one of them:

> But he rose upon their decks and he cried,
> I have fought for Queen and faith like a valiant man and true;
> I have only done my duty as a man is bound to do.
> With a joyful spirit I Sir Richard Grenville die.

The Spaniards, too, who praised him to his face with their courtly foreign grace, are in the true Plutarchian tradition. The great conqueror shows magnanimity to the conquered. Alexander was "as gentle after victory as he was terrible on the field." In the Life of Aemilius Paulus when he was told that the leader of the enemy's

forces had surrendered and had asked to be taken to
him, "he rose from his seat and accompanied by his
friends went himself to meet him with tears in his eyes
for a formidable opponent who had failed." The war
with him had cost the Romans much, but a defeated foe
ceased to be an enemy. "When the invincible and terrible
Hannibal was vanquished," Plutarch says, "Scipio gave
him his hand and put no hard article in the peace treaty,
nor insulted him in his fallen fortune." The Victorian
poets understood that point of honor as well as Plutarch
did — learned it from him very likely along with Sir
Thomas Malory. When "the Dane" was conquered in
the Battle of the Baltic,

> Outspake the victor then
> As he hailed them o'er the wave,
> Ye are brothers! Ye are men!
> And we conquer but to save: —
> So peace instead of death let us bring.

We seem today to be establishing a new tradition of the
way the victor should treat the vanquished. If it is to
prevail, Plutarch will be carefully censored along with
the Victorians.

Plutarch called himself a Platonist. His bent of mind,
however, was more Socratic than Platonic. He wanted
to do what Cicero said Socrates had done, "bring philosophy down from heaven into the cities and the homes

of men." In his hands, as he talked to his friends in Chaeronea, in Delphi, divine philosophy took on a pleasantly homely look. It was said of Socrates that to him knowledge, philosophy, was "action getting under way." That was exactly Plutarch's idea. Philosophy must work in daily life to guide men in the path to virtuous action.

He stood at the beginning of a new era in religion and he felt that it was so and that he was part of it, but he did not let go of the old, of what he calls, "the ancient and hereditary faith." The different gods were merely different views of the one God, perfect in goodness, or perhaps they were different ways of trying to find Him. The myths, he said, were "to be tenderly treated," interpreted in "a spirit at once pious and philosophic." They are, he writes, the reflection of truth like "the rainbow which the mathematicians tell us is nothing else but an image of the sun, a reflection of his beams upon the clouds." Nevertheless he knew that the framework which always encloses religion was falling apart and a new frame had to be constructed.

A startling change was taking place before his eyes. A great religious institution was coming to an end, the oracles were failing. They had been very important. Through them men had had the assurance of direct communication with God. In great distresses and perplexities it was possible to find out what should be done. They could get divine counsel at Delphi, at Argos, as

far away as Ammon's temple in the Sahara. But everywhere oracles were ceasing to speak. Why? men were
asking. Plutarch answers the question in a remarkable
passage. He could be a clear, hard thinker on occasion.
The oracle at Delphi, he points out, depended on two
things, the vapor in the Delphic cave and the priestess
who spoke under its influence. Neither was divine. They
operated according to natural law and were subject, as
all things in nature, to change and decay. The power
behind the oracles was God, but in speaking by means
of them He used what was fallible and imperfect. His
words came to men not directly, but through natural
channels. "God," Plutarch sums up, "is not a ventrilo-
quist."

A statement like that shakes the condescension with
which we view the pre-Christian world. An infallible
voice, an infallibly dictated Book — a large part of the
western world today holds to the one or the other, each
a manifestation of God's powerful ventriloquism.

A man who thought like this could not be super-
stitious. Plutarch had no tolerance for that particular
form of human weakness. To him a superstition was not
a mistaken belief, a kind of religious stupidity; it was an
unmitigated evil, far worse than absolute disbelief. Athe-
ism, he says, denies God, but superstition wrongs Him.
It makes God evil or silly. It uses the very worst of all
weapons, terror. It fills the world after death with "flam-

ing fires and awful shapes and inexorable judges and horrible torments"; in this world it teaches people to practice absurd penances and self-torturing. Better far not to see God at all than see Him like that. "I had rather have it said that there was not and never had been such a fellow as Plutarch, than that he was fickle and vindictive and would pay you out for not calling upon him."

His religious creed was not complicated. A contemporary of his, the younger Pliny, wrote, "For man to help man is God," and to Plutarch that was certainly a clause in the definition. The life according to God was accepting an unconditional obligation to make things better for others wherever one was. But there was more than that. In an essay he wrote upon the delay of God in punishing the wicked he faced with candor and with courage the basic problem of religion, the problem of evil. He did not propose a solution. With our limited knowledge, to try to understand God's ways was, he said, like a man's looking at a painting and claiming to be able to explain how it was done because he had analyzed the colors and knew how they were mixed. Nevertheless, in God's slowness to punish there was a clue to understanding Him. He gives people time to repent, and from Him we may learn patience with those who wrong us and forgiveness.

Of course as a Platonist he believed in the reality

and the eternity of the things not seen, but the Greeks for generations before him had been learning Platonic idealism through hard facts. Ever since Alexander's day they had been forced to see that the things that are seen are temporal; they vanish, riches, power, empire, no matter how solidly founded, how mightily bulwarked, and only the splendor of the spirit endures.

The immortality of the soul necessarily followed or, rather, was bound up in this conception. Life and death, Plutarch says, are only the prelude to the great initiation. We are like those being initiated into the mysteries. At first they wander along tortuous ways and through wearisome mazes, which end in a shuddering passage through darkness full of terror. But then "a clear shining light comes to meet you; pure meadows receive you; there is song and dance and holy apparitions." In the letter he writes to his wife about the death of their little daughter, he says, "About that which you have heard, dear heart, that the soul once departed from the body vanishes and feels nothing, I know that you give no belief to such assertions because of those sacred and faithful promises given in the mysteries of Dionysus which we who are of that religious brotherhood know. We hold it firmly for an undoubted truth that our soul is incorruptible and immortal. We are to think [of the dead] that they pass to a better place and a happier condition. Let us behave ourselves accordingly, outwardly by an ordered life, while within all should be pure, wise, incorruptible."

"Is God so petty," he asks, "so attached to the trifling, that He will take the trouble to create souls if we have nothing divine in us, nothing that resembles Him, nothing lasting or sure, but all of us fades like a leaf?"

The unseen world was peopled for him with hosts of spirits, good and bad, but chiefly good. The bad were useful in lifting from God the burden of responsibility for evil, and the good satisfied the human longing for a mediator between God's awful perfection and man's feeble wickedness. They were the spirits of good men who, Plutarch says, "have become able to share in the nature of God." They could draw near to men and help them. If a man persists on the path of excellence, he will become "able to hear this spiritual speech which fills all the air but can be heard only by those whose souls are pure."

Plutarch was not an original or profound thinker. He could not melt the old in the fire and fuse it into a new form. But he was typically Greek. In that age of confusion when the young Christian Church first confronted the classic world he could and did hold up the bright torch of the Greek spirit so soon to be darkened for centuries to come. Christianity in its beginnings was addressed to Greeks. The Gospels as we have them are in Greek. St. Paul wrote in Greek to Greek-speaking Christians. Plutarch never came into contact with the new religion; he knew nothing about Christianity, although his spirit was naturally Christian, as was said of Socrates. But when Christianity entered Greece it must have made converts of many men like Plutarch, spiritually minded, longing for light, men of strong mentality too. But, extraordinarily, the Church was never really influenced by Greeks. Two roads lay open to her, the Greek way and the Roman way, and she took the Roman. It was a decisive choice, destined to affect fundamentally the course of Christianity.

Chapter X

THE GREEK WAY AND
THE ROMAN WAY

THE INFLUENCE of Greece and the power of Greek thought is generally passed over in any account of the beginning of the Christian Church for the reason that it was powerful only at the beginning and came to an end quickly. In those first years two roads lay open before the Church, the Greek way and the Roman way. They were distinct from each other; they had few points of contact. Inevitably the way of the Church would incline to one or the other because they were the two great powers in the world she faced, each a great power, but not in the same sense. Rome was the ruler of the world, Greece a small country she had conquered, an insignificant bit of the immense empire. That was one point of view, but there was another. Spiritually, in the world of thought and art, Greece was the ruler. The Romans acknowledged it. "Captive Greece has taken captive her conqueror," a Latin poet wrote. Nothing shows the Romans in a better light than that they recognized their own intellectual and spiritual inferiority and were able to learn from a helpless, subject nation. Greece in her fashion was as powerful as Rome in the world where the Christian Church began.

Just at first the Church took the Greek way. The New Testament is written in Greek. The leaders of the little Christian centers — there was not yet one Church — were Greeks or educated by Greeks. But that was a condition which did not last long. The Roman way quickly proved to be more attractive and it is easy to see why. In the world the Church faced, the forces of evil were so overwhelmingly powerful it was most difficult to hold fast to the Christian faith that the only power which mattered, the only power which endured, was spiritual power. In face of the Roman Empire it seemed to the world at large a feeble thing. But the Greeks had been learning for generations that the things that are seen are temporal. They had had to give them up, one after another. They were a poverty-stricken, conquered country; their freedom was lost, their independence gone, but the things that are not seen were still theirs; their rule over men's spirits and minds still remained. They had seen for themselves that no dependence could be placed on any material good. The welfare that prosperity brings was never to be counted on. Only the things not seen were sure. How well they had learned that lesson their later writers show, especially the greatest, Plutarch.

The suffering which had taught it to them had impressed it ineffaceably upon their minds and for them it was easy to understand Christ's rejection in the desert of the kingdoms of the world and the glory of them. If the Church had chosen the Greek way she would have found Christ's way far easier and she might with Him have disdained temporal power. But she chose the Roman way.

The times were dark and perilous and it was almost inevitable that the little scattered centers of Christian living should turn for leadership to the strongest and most authoritative. That was the church in Rome, an admirably disciplined and notably effective body. In comparison what were the Greeks? Thinkers and artists, the world called them then as now. Thought and art are the products not of a powerful working force, a mass of men acting together, but of separate individuals going their own different ways. People like that will never be dependably efficient. Even in their very best days the Greeks could never make a Greek Empire. They did not really like working together; they wanted freedom to do as each one pleased. But to the Romans union was strength, and that was what mattered. Mind and spirit — they were fairly negligible. What was important was the will. When Christ said, "Seek and ye shall find," and "Ye shall know the truth and the truth shall set you free," He said what was easy for a Greek to understand, but very hard for a Roman. The Romans were wonderful organizers, and an organization is not a place where people are encouraged to seek or to be free.

To the Romans the first essentials were obedience to authority and disciplined control, as was natural to a nation which Livy said had been at war for eight hundred years. "Like a mighty army moves the Church of God." That is a Roman, not a Greek idea. There is no praise in Greek literature for unquestioning obedience or for doing and saying and thinking what everyone else does. The Greeks wanted independent citizens who thought for themselves; the Romans distrusted anyone who was different and wanted citizens who were not given to thinking, but to doing what they were told.

So the young Christian Church turned from the Greek way and chose the Roman way. No more little communities of Christians each led by the Spirit of Truth which Christ had promised them. The Romans with their genius for organization took them over and built up one great institution so superbly planned and developed that it finally was able to step into the place of the Roman Empire. Never could that magnificent position have been reached by following the Greek way.

The Roman way led the Church to supreme power, power over heaven and hell as well as the earth.

All power tends to corrupt, Lord Acton said as Plato had said before him. Thucydides had said that all power thirsts for more power. The more authoritative the Church grew, the more authority she claimed over more and more people. Underlying her whole conception of dealing with mankind was an idea congenial and familiar to Romans and foreign to Greeks. The Romans thought poorly of human nature. It was tolerable only when under strong control. Humanity was evil throughout. This was far from the Greek way. From the beginning the Greeks had had a vision of what St. John, the Greek thinker among the Evangelists, called "the true light which lighteth every man that cometh into the world" — "the divine," the Odyssey says, "for which all men long." Socrates' fundamental conviction was that there was in everyone a spark of the divine light which could be kindled into a flame. In his speech to his judges just before they condemned him to death he said: "I will obey God rather than you, and as long as I have breath I will not cease from exhorting you: 'My friend, are you not ashamed of caring so much about making money and about reputation and honors? Will you not think or care about wisdom and truth and how to make your soul better? I shall reproach you for indifference to what is most valuable and prizing what is unimportant. I shall do this to everyone I meet, young and old, for this is God's command to me.'" He never told them what wisdom and truth were. All he did was to ask them questions, but his questions led them into the depths of themselves where he knew the spark could be found and kindled.

Plato repeated over and over again that the knowledge of God, the source of all good to men, could be reached only because there was "a kindred power in the soul." He writes, "A gentle and noble nature who desires all truth and who seeks to be like God as far as that is possible for man ... is the happiest man. He is a royal man, king over himself. Even when he is in poverty or sickness or any other seeming misfortune, all things will in the end work together for good to him in life and in death.

"Wherefore my counsel is that we hold fast ever to the heavenly way and follow after justice and excellence always, considering that the soul is immortal. Thus shall we live dear to one another and to the gods, both here and when, like conquerors in the games, we receive our reward."

"God knows," Plutarch says, "with how great a share of goodness souls come into the world, how strong is their nobility of nature which they derive from Him Himself. And if they do break out into vice, corrupted by bad habits and bad companions, they may yet reform."

Christ's last prayer had been "Father, forgive them for they know not what they do." Plutarch would have understood that prayer.

In Rome the influences were not for mercy and pity. Cicero, as kind a man as could well be found there, writes a friend about some specially spectacular gladiatorial games he had been to: "They were magnificent — and yet what real pleasure can a cultivated person get from watching a puny man being mangled by a tremendously powerful beast? Still, the games *are* an incomparable training in making the spectators despise suffering and death." But Athens never admitted the gladiatorial games. There is a story that once when the Assembly was considering a proposal for gladiators to come and stage one of their contests, a man sprang to his feet and cried, "Athenians, before we invite the gladiators come with me and tear down the temple to Pity." He won the day. They voted unanimously to reject the gladiators. In all Athens' history, Socrates was the only man put to death for his opinions. His executioners killed him by giving him a poison that made him die with no pain. They were Greeks. The Romans hung Christ upon a cross.

If the Church had chosen the Greek way some of the most terrible pages in history might never have had to be written. The Inquisition, the prisons people were flung into, the ways the condemned were killed, the massacres of nonconformists — all this was fostered and favored by the conviction that human beings generally were bad and ought to suffer. The conception of God which developed through these ruthless centuries was calculated to do away with mercy and compassion in the hearts of His worshipers. It is phrased clearly in the Westminster Shorter Catechism, a subject for reverential study in Presbyterian households for hundreds of years. In it this statement is made: In Adam's fall "mankind lost communion with God, are under His wrath and curses, and so made liable to all the miseries of this life, to death itself, and to the pains of hell for ever." If God felt that way it was clearly right for men to make objectionable people suffer. Whatever they did would be less than the pains of hell forever; men need not be more merciful and pitiful than God. If the Church had taken the Greek way that weight of human agony might never have been. A cruel God would not have been possible to Greeks.

Another danger too might well have been avoided, less great but yet of major importance, the danger of formalism, of considering the outside more important than the inside, of holding up a form of words, a creed or theology, as a more basic expression of the truth than the way people live. Christ said, "Ye shall know them by their fruits."

That is not the way the Church went. The Inquisition put people to death not for living wickedly, but for making what to the Inquisitors were incorrect statements. The Greeks were not interested in trying to make correct statements about the infinite and the eternal. Plato said, "To find the father and maker of all is hard and having found him it is impossible to utter him," and he speaks of truth coming to him suddenly like a flame blazing up from a spark. That flame shrivels up formalism.

Socrates had his inner certainties, but they were not expressed as clear assertions, and just because he did not try to imprison the truth in a formula his truth has lived. The Gospels will be searched in vain for a definition of God. Christ never gave any. He called Him our Father; He spoke of the love of God; He told the parable of the prodigal son; but He never put into a definite statement what God is. He said, The truth shall make you free, but He did not say, This is the truth. There is no clearly defined creed in the Gospels. Here again Christ's way was the way natural to the Greeks. It was the Roman way to make an authoritative declaration about the things unseen and have it received without question.

The Greek way was marked out also by not being ever the easy way. "Excellence much labored for by the race of men," says Aristotle. One of the earliest Greek poets says, "Before the gates of excellence the high gods have placed sweat. Long is the road thereto and rough and steep." Another poet says that a man must suffer "heart-grieving sweat" to produce anything that is of value, and Plato says, "Hard is the good."

No one ever called the way Christ himself walked the easy way. He said, "Strait is the gate, and narrow is the way, which leadeth unto life, and few there be that find it." There could hardly be a greater denial of the Christian way than to represent it as broad and smooth and leading to a happy success, but when times are very prosperous and comfortable a tendency to easy religion develops and then the Greek way can reinforce the way of Christ. It would have been inconceivable to Socrates, to Plato, to the Stoics, that a result of religion could be a prosperous life. Virtue is its own reward, the Stoics said. The only reward of serving God, Plato said, was to become able to serve Him better.

Prosperity as a reward for obeying God's command never entered Socrates' mind. He told his judges in court after the sentence of death was pronounced, "I see clearly that the time has come when it is better for me to die, and so my accusers have done me no harm.

Still — they did not mean to do me good and for this I may gently blame them. And now we go our ways, you to live and I to die. Which is better only God knows." A friend who was with him in the prison cell when he drank the poison, told another, "I could not pity him. He seemed to me beyond that. I thought of him as blessed." Socrates had his reward.

A day or two before his death when a rich man who knew he could bribe the jailers and get Socrates away, came to him begging, "Let us save you, Socrates, your friends beseech you," Socrates said, "Dear Crito, a voice within me is telling me that I must not disobey my country's laws and do what is wrong in order to save my life. It is very loud, this voice, so that I can hardly hear another's. Yet if you wish to say more, speak and I will listen." "Socrates, I have nothing more to say." "Then, leave me, Crito, to obey the will of God."

What would it not have meant to the religion of Christ if Christians had been learners as well as teachers of Greece. The basic Greek idea that nothing of value can be easily won would have found a perfect fulfillment in Christ's life. The cruelties practiced in his name might not — almost surely would not — have defaced the religion of love. There would have been, too, another criterion of the truth, not only creeds and *ipse dixits* authoritatively promulgated and obediently accepted, but

Plutarch's criterion, If we live here as we ought, we shall see things as they are, the Greek version of, The pure in heart shall see God.

"The excellent becomes the permanent." The influence of Greece died, but the truth and the beauty the Greeks discovered finally came to life again and have never passed away. They are still our teachers.